# BECOMING
# GOD'S
# VESSEL
## OF
# HONOR

# BECOMING
# GOD'S
# VESSEL
## OF
# HONOR

## LESSIE
## HARVEY

ACW Press
Ozark, AL 36360

**Becoming God's Vessel of Honor**
Copyright ©2005 Lessie Harvey
All rights reserved

Cover Design by Alpha Advertising
Interior Design by Pine Hill Graphics

Packaged by ACW Press
1200 HWY 231 South #273
Ozark, AL 36360
www.acwpress.com
The views expressed or implied in this work do not necessarily reflect those of ACW Press. Ultimate design, content, and editorial accuracy of this work is the responsibility of the author(s).

Library of Congress Cataloging-in-Publication Data
*(Provided by Cassidy Cataloguing Services, Inc.)*

Harvey, Lessie.

Becoming God's vessel of honor / Lessie Harvey. — 1st ed. — Ozark, AL : ACW Press, 2005.

p. ; cm.

Includes bibliographical references.
ISBN: 1-932124-63-2

1. Christian women—Religious life. 2. Christian women—Conduct of life. 3. Christian life. 4. Spiritual life—Christianity. I. Title.

BV4527 .H37 2005
248.8/43—dc22                                     0506

**Printed in the United States of America.**

*This book is dedicated to my family,
friends, and all who encouraged me to
pursue and fulfill my dreams.*

# Acknowledgments

Special thanks to Florence and Marita Littauer, the UpperCLASS staff, and all who attended UpperCLASS with me. Thanks for helping me to realize my "speech" was a book in disguise. Thanks to Veda Shaw for continued encouragement after the class.

The insight from my readers was invaluable. Many thanks to: Micheal Washington, Dorisann Tarver, Chrissandra Alexander, Paulette Wages, Beth Radford, Zeleana Morris, and Pastor Donald Leon Smedley.

To those who allowed me to share my thoughts and/or offered suggestions, I am grateful. Many thanks to: Saundra Bates, Cheron Wicker, Johnell Washington, Dave Washington Jr., Jacqueline Jones, Vina Coleman, Haskell and Anne Harvey, Ifeoma Ezekwo, Lauren Briggs, Curtis Forward, Jane Roach, Claire DeBakey, Noreen Alexander, Colin MacLachlan, Lauren Terry, Debbi Anceravage, Sandra Grace, Kim Bunton, Larry and Dee Taylor, Rhonda Richard, Kathy Culmer, Caren Howard, Tiffany Harvey, Johnathan Harvey, Varian Harvey, and Jesse Harvey.

The critique and editing skills of Susan Titus Osborn are fantastic! Thanks Susan for giving me a reader's perspective and a joy for rewriting.

Thanks Martha Spittal for helping me to understand the nuances between words and to concisely express my thoughts.

Finally, thanks Wayne Hastings for giving me the courage to create a path for myself and to move forward when I attended the Glorieta Christian Writer's Conference. Also, thanks Jack Cavanaugh for understanding my needs and suggesting that I contact ACW Press. Thanks Chuck Dean and Julie Wood at ACW Press for your patience and kindness. Thanks to Fred Renich at Pine Hill Graphics for making my dream a reality.

# CONTENTS

Foreword . . . . . . . . . . . . . . . . . . . . . . . . . . . . . . . . . . . . . . . . . . . . . 9

Introduction . . . . . . . . . . . . . . . . . . . . . . . . . . . . . . . . . . . . . . . . . 11

CHAPTER 1

Clarity Regarding God's Vessels . . . . . . . . . . . . . . . . . . . . . . . 15
*What is This Thing Called Salvation? / Jesus' Role in
Salvation / Our Status Before a Holy God / The Importance
of Commitment / Trust is the Foundation / Jesus as Lord /
Are You Known by Jesus?*

CHAPTER 2

Clay Vessels: Hard to Distinguish From the World . . . . . . . 29
*No Distinction from the World / Faith in God, not Self or
Others / Wavering in Our Walk / Choosing to Obey God /
Sanctified Clay Vessel*

CHAPTER 3

Don't Give Up! . . . . . . . . . . . . . . . . . . . . . . . . . . . . . . . . . . . . . 43
*The Purpose of Trials / Weariness in Doing Right / Hope
Kindles Perseverance*

CHAPTER 4

Wooden Vessels: Overcoming Others with Scripture . . . . . . 59
*Scribes and Pharisees Mentality / Paul, Before the Damascus
Road Experience / Paul, After the Damascus Road
Experience / Why We Need God's Holy Spirit*

CHAPTER 5

Problems: Who Needs Them! . . . . . . . . . . . . . . . . . . . . . . . . 73
*Submission Defined / The "Me" Factor / Godly Submission /
Why God Chastens / Commitment Determines Submission /
Submission Unto Death*

CHAPTER 6
Silver Vessels: You're Beginning to Shine . . . . . . . . . . . . . . . . 91
*What Happened to the Good Life?*

CHAPTER 7
Surrendering to God. . . . . . . . . . . . . . . . . . . . . . . . . . . . . . . 105
*Surrender Based on Love / Trust / Faith / Fellowship*

CHAPTER 8
Golden Vessels: A Pleasing Aroma to God . . . . . . . . . . . . . . 115
*Committed and Disciplined / Godliness / Intercession /*
*A Pleasing Aroma*

CHAPTER 9
They Chose to Serve . . . . . . . . . . . . . . . . . . . . . . . . . . . . . . . 129
*People Who Made a Difference / Division in the Body*

Endnotes . . . . . . . . . . . . . . . . . . . . . . . . . . . . . . . . . . . . . . . . 139

# FOREWORD

Every Christian woman wants a closer relationship with God. The question is: How do we achieve that goal? In this book, Lessie Harvey uses clay, wood, silver, and gold vessels as examples of an individual's spiritual growth. The desire to seek a personal relationship with God is the first step. Our spiritual growth, however, shouldn't stop there. As clay vessels, we need to allow God to mold us into His image if we are to become useful to Him.

As we learn to seek God and to trust Him in the midst of our problems, we become vessels of wood. When we submit to His leading and truly believe in Him, we will allow Him to chisel our wooden vessels to His liking. We need to realize that He has our best interests at heart, but it's not until God carves His will on our hearts that we become valuable and can make a difference in the lives of those around us.

Next God asks us to allow Him to put us through the refiner's fire to melt away the dross, the sinful ways that are not of Him. Refined silver reflects the face of the One who refines it. At this point, godly qualities can be seen in the silver vessel.

Through studying Scripture, coming to God in prayer, worshipping with other believers, and living a life pleasing to God, we receive further refinement, and we become golden vessels. Then we have completed our journey and achieved our goal of becoming vessels of honor, sanctified and useful to the Master. And that is when God can use us to encourage others to also become God's Vessels of Honor.

*Susan Titus Osborn*
Director of the Christian Communicator Manuscript Critique Service
Author of 28 books

*Now in a large house there are not only gold and silver vessels, but also vessels of wood and (clay), and some to honor and some to dishonor. Therefore, if a man cleanses himself from these things, he will be a vessel for honor, sanctified, useful to the Master, prepared for every good work.*

2 Timothy 2:20-21 (NAS)

Before entering her car, Martha turned around and took a long look at the church building where her Bible study group had met. She closed her eyes. Hot tears spilled onto her cheeks.

"God, I don't understand why You did not allow the class to continue. I worked hard getting the class started. People were coming. They loved studying Your Word. What happened? What went wrong?"

"Martha," said her friend, Lilly, from the passenger side of the car, "don't blame yourself. You know that all things work together for good for those who love God and are called according to His purpose" (Romans 8:28).

"I know," said Martha, "but it still hurts." She sat in her seat, fastened her seatbelt, turned on the ignition, and drove away—in silence.

Daily we make choices. Some are good. Some are bad. As long as our good choices outnumber our bad ones, we may feel that all is well—that life is good and we are in control.

Regardless of how good we may think our lives are, apart from a relationship with God, we are vessels of dishonor with little or no purpose on earth.

Salvation—believing Jesus is God and accepting Him as our Savior and Lord—makes us vessels of honor. Although we have value to God, seldom can others see our value, because our transformation process is invisible.

Genesis 2:7 says that God formed us out of the dust of the ground. The exterior color of one's clay may be different from another's, but we all come from the same thing: dust. That is why it is hard to distinguish new believers from those who don't know Christ as their Savior. A new believer is just beginning her walk with God. Since she has not yet learned to love, trust, or submit to Him, she may still act as she did when she did not know God.

A worldly believer, although professing to know, love, and serve God, still chooses to be her own god. Therefore she places her needs and her desires above God's will. Her self-centered lifestyle has little or no godly impact on others because she is just like them.

Salvation makes us more than just vessels of honor. It opens the door for God to begin His transformation process in our lives. As clay vessels we may resemble those in the world, but God is working within us, conforming us into the image of His Son.

Once saved, we must persevere in our desire to know Christ in all His fullness. We must choose to study the Bible, fellowship with other believers, worship God, and pray.

Learning Scripture should be a priority in our lives. Not for boasting or belittling others but for allowing the Holy Spirit to use God's Word to teach, rebuke, or correct us, as well as to use it to minister to other people God brings across our paths.

It is not enough merely to know Scripture. Satan knows Scripture, but he is not using it to draw others into the kingdom of God. (See Matthew 4:1-11.) Instead, we must yield the use of Scripture to God's Holy Spirit. When God's Word is engraved upon our hearts, He can wield the Sword of the Spirit in a way that is fruitful in bringing others into His kingdom. It is the power of His Word that draws others to Him, not our power. We are instruments that He uses to bring others into His kingdom.

Outwardly we have not changed, but inwardly we experience transformation. As wooden vessels, we memorize Scripture, engraving it upon our minds. God's Spirit is then able to take what we have learned and give us understanding. We are no longer the people we were when we accepted Christ as Savior and Lord.

The transformation process does not stop there. Once we have passed the salvation phase as clay vessels and persevered through learning Scripture and engraving it upon our hearts as wooden vessels, we then come to the submission phase of the silver vessel.

Many of us have problems with submission. In fact, the word "submission" has a negative connotation to most people. If we are to continue our transformation progress, we must view submission in a different light. We must first submit to God. If not, true submission to others is not possible over the long haul.

God refines us as silver vessels by testing our willingness to submit to difficult circumstances. We will either submit to God's will, trusting that He is in control and seeking to do what pleases Him, or trust ourselves and do what we think is best in a situation.

Only the Refiner knows that which He is refining. He sees what needs to be done and does it. Purity is His goal. To endure the refining process, we must trust the Refiner. Anything less leads to impure silver, which is of little value to the Refiner. The transformation process is slowed when we are no longer in submission to God. True submission comes from a heart that trusts God and is committed to Him, regardless of circumstances.

In the final phase of the transformation process, the golden vessel signifies complete surrender to God. Once we have reached this state, we no longer question why God has allowed certain things in our lives. Our focus is no longer on self, but on God and others.

As golden vessels, our goal is not perfection but rather intercession. Our prayers give God the opportunity to freely work in all areas of our lives. As the temple priests entered the holy of holies offering an aroma pleasing to God, we too can offer pleasing aromas as we intercede on behalf of others.

Martha was disappointed that the Bible study class she helped start ended after six weeks. Yet, she was ready for God's refining fire. Her submission to God's will, not her own, showed her true heart for God.

As God tested Martha, so will He test all who belong to Him as we grow in our relationship with Him. But what a privilege to be worked on by God, and through salvation, perseverance, submission, and complete surrender, we can become vessels of honor, sanctified and useful to the Master.

# CHAPTER ONE

# Identifying God's Vessels

## Salvation

Every Sunday, our church service closes with a threefold invitation to the congregation. The first is for those who have not accepted Christ as their Savior. The second is for those who want to publicly profess Christ as their Savior, and the third is for those who are looking for a church home and want to join our church. I've done all three, but I still don't feel close to God," confided Wanda to her friend Lisa.

Lisa nodded her head in agreement. "I've felt that way too. That's why I joined a weekly Bible study group. As I learn about God, I don't feel as distant from Him."

"Do you think I should spend more time at church or volunteer to work on a committee?"

"Instead of working on another committee," Lisa replied, "maybe you should begin reading your Bible regularly. And perhaps you should come to Bible study with me. We can learn together and discuss what we've read."

"I've tried reading my Bible daily, but something always comes up, or I completely forget to read. How can I find time to add a Bible study class to my already hectic schedule? God knows me, and He knows how I feel about Him."

"Wanda, I know God knows you. He made you! But do you know Him? How can you feel close to someone you don't know? Before you married Bill, remember how much time you spent with him? Would you have married him if you didn't know him?"

"That's different. If I didn't spend time getting to know Bill, I wouldn't have felt comfortable marrying him. God knows me and loves me. He accepts me as I am. Bill didn't know me or love me. Spending time together was necessary to build a relationship. How else would we have gotten to know one another?'"

"Wanda, how are relationships built? It's true that God knows you and loves you, but do you know God or truly love Him? How can you know Him without reading the Bible and meditating on what it says to discover who He is and what He expects from someone who loves Him? A relationship involves a commitment from both sides, not just one person."

"Ummm, Lisa. I've never thought about it like that. Do you really think God expects me to commit to Him in a relationship? Am I to trust Him with everything in my life? What if I don't like how things are going? Who am I going to complain to?"

---

Wanda's concerns are valid, especially when we begin our walk with God. Second Timothy 2:20-21 says:

*In a large house there are not only gold and silver vessels, but also vessels of wood and of [clay], and some to honor and some to dishonor. Therefore, if a man cleanses himself from these things, he will be a vessel for honor, sanctified, useful to the Master, prepared for every good work (NAS).*

We all come to God in our natural state—clay. There is no difference between us and others God has made. Only when we respond to His call to us are we on a different path from those around us. God can then begin to mold us as we submit to Him.

An artist is limited by his creative ability when molding clay. God has greater creative ability than any artist on earth. He knows exactly what He has created each of us to be. Therefore we need to know and trust the God who made us so we can become all He has created us to be.

As we read Scripture, we learn about God and are eager to share what we learn with our friends and loved ones. This could be called our wooden state because during this time God's word is carved on our hearts. We may have plenty of head knowledge about God, but few of us know how to apply Scripture to our lives.

After God's word is engraved upon our hearts, He usually allows trials in our lives to reveal our true heart toward Him to ourselves. It is usually during this time that we realize we are not a good reflection of God because of sin in our lives. Although our desire is to please God, we must see ourselves as He sees us and willingly submit to His refining process.

During difficulties, we discover how close we are to God, or how far we are from Him. This is our silver state because the refining process gives us the opportunity to discard all that is not of God in our lives. We may choose to hold onto certain areas of sin in our lives, but they only block God's reflection from being seen by others in us. Either we are transparent so that others can see God in us, or we cling to our sin and become impure silver.

Our clay, wooden, and silver states should prepare us for our golden state. At this point in our lives, we not only accept what God allows in our lives, but we consider it an honor to intercede on behalf of others, whether they request it or not. Focus is no longer on self, but rather on God's purpose for our lives.

In order to reach the golden state and become vessels of honor, we need to have the right foundation. Our walk with God truly begins with salvation. Submission to God and perseverance during difficulties make us pliable and moldable so we may become vessels of honor, sanctified, useful to the Master.

## WHAT IS THIS THING CALLED SALVATION?

In our journey toward *Becoming God's Vessel of Honor,* we must first consider our response to the salvation message—accepting Jesus as our Lord and Savior.

*Vine's Complete Expository Dictionary of Old and New Testament Words* defines salvation as: "The spiritual and eternal deliverance granted immediately by God to those who accept His conditions of repentance and faith in the Lord Jesus, in whom alone it is to be obtained (Acts 4:12) and upon confession of Him as Lord (Romans 10:10)."

Acts 4:12 says, "Salvation is found in no one else, for there is no other name under heaven given to men by which we must be saved."

The Romans Scripture states, "For it is with your heart that you believe and are justified, and it is with your mouth that you confess and are saved."

Webster's theological definition is: "Deliverance from sin and penalty, realized in a future state; redemption."

Both definitions focus on deliverance. Therefore, we must first prayerfully realize that we need to be delivered from something—alcohol, debt, lust, greed, gossip, and working too much are some examples. These are just outward symptoms of the underlying disease—self-centeredness. A person may seem to be outwardly righteous and still be a self-centered sinner.

Once that realization is made, we must then realize if we are capable of freeing ourselves from the situation. If not, then we need to decide to trust someone else who has the ability to bring about freedom for us.

Trusting someone to free us from a burden that binds is not a simple matter. It is usually at this point that we look for the best possible solution to our problems. Friends are consulted, viable solutions are researched, and tentative plans are made to bring deliverance. However, earthly solutions do not bring spiritual freedom when we fall short of fulfilling the requirements set by God.

Good works cannot erase the distance between a holy God and sinful people, nor can a good moral life, regular church attendance, or generous giving fill the chasm that separates individuals from God.

Only when we cease to look horizontally, and instead choose to look vertically to compare ourselves to a holy God, will we begin to realize that we are in need of deliverance spiritually. When we look horizontally, we can always find someone worse than ourselves. However, when we look vertically and acknowledge our true standing before a holy God, we realize that God is always greater and that no earthly accomplishment can be compared to Him.

Only when we see ourselves spiritually lacking does salvation become a personal need, especially if we desire to be in God's presence for eternity. But what does Christ have to do with salvation? Is He the only way?

## JESUS' ROLE IN SALVATION

John 1:1 says, "In the beginning was the Word, and the Word was with God, and the Word was God." John refers to Jesus as the personal manifestation of God in the flesh. Understanding that Jesus is God, the second Person of the Trinity, is one of the most important concepts to grasp if we are going to choose to believe in Jesus as Savior and Lord.

Lessie Harvey says of her life before her salvation: "I struggled with the deity of Jesus because I did not believe in middlemen. I felt adequate in presenting my requests to God the Father, and I trusted Him to respond favorably on my behalf. However, I did not value Jesus, because I did not understand His relationship to God the Father or His role in creation or salvation."

It is easy for us to invite Jesus into our lives, but until we understand His role as Savior, we may continue to live life as before—depending upon ourselves or other people. When Adam and Eve sinned, all who came after them were born in sin. The only exception is Jesus Christ. He never sinned, and He never turned away from doing that which He was sent to do. Jesus says in John 17:1-5:

> *Father, the time has come. Glorify your Son, that your Son may glorify you. For you granted him authority over all people that he might give eternal life to all those you have given him. Now this is eternal life: that they may know you, the only true God, and Jesus Christ, whom you have sent. I have brought you glory on earth by completing the work you*

*gave me to do. And now, Father, glorify me in your presence*
*with the glory I had with you before the world began.*

No person can make that claim because all have sinned. There
have been good people, but good people cannot, on the strength of
their goodness, stand in the presence of a holy God.

Jesus remained true to God the Father while He lived on earth.
He chose to die so that He could set free all of us bound by sin. He
is the only sacrifice God the Father accepts, according to 1
Corinthians 15:56-57: "The sting of death is sin, and the power of
sin is the law. But thanks be to God! He gives us the victory through
our Lord Jesus Christ."

Therefore, Jesus Christ is above all people and has done what
no other man on earth can do—bridge the gap between a holy God
and His sinful people. Only through Jesus can we restore the broken relationship with God.

Jesus is God and has all the Father's attributes. In other words,
He has the same inherent characteristics as God. Yet, Jesus became
man and thus can relate to us.

Because Jesus is God and man, earthly beings are not His equal.
According to Philippians 2:9-11: "Therefore God exalted him to the
highest place and gave him the name that is above every name, that
at the name of Jesus every knee should bow, in heaven, and on
earth and under the earth, and every tongue confess that Jesus
Christ is Lord, to the glory of God the Father."

When we understand who Jesus is and why He died on the
cross, then we are ready to make a heart, not head, decision by fully
committing ourselves to Him and trusting in Him.

## OUR STATUS BEFORE A HOLY GOD

Romans 3:23 states, "For all have sinned and fall short of the
glory of God," and 6:23 says, "For the wages of sin is death." These
verses are offensive to some, especially those who live good moral
lives. As long as people see themselves as good, they are not interested in salvation. Why should they seek salvation, when they think
they are in control?

When our lives spiral out of control, we assume it is a temporary situation. As long as we believe we have the ability to make decisions that can extinguish inflammatory circumstances, resolve hurtful problems, or restore personal control and harmony, we don't see a need to look beyond ourselves for help.

God's answer to our dilemma is found in Romans 5:8: "But God demonstrates his own love for us in this: While we were still sinners, Christ died for us."

Mankind's fall into sin is recorded in Genesis 3, when Adam and Eve ate from the tree of the knowledge of good and evil. God provided the remedy for sin in Genesis 3:15, when He told the serpent that the woman's offspring would crush the serpent's head. Even though we must suffer the consequences of sin, God provided the way of escape from a life of sin through belief in Jesus and acceptance of His death on the cross as the substitutionary payment for our sin.

Unless we are willing to acknowledge our righteous deeds as filthy rags before a holy God, we cannot enter into a true relationship of commitment and trust in God.

## THE IMPORTANCE OF COMMITMENT

A relationship becomes serious when the people involved make a commitment to one another. They feel they are entrusting themselves to the care of someone who has their best interests at heart. They don't fear or doubt as they enter into their relationship because trust is their foundation.

Even when one of them does not understand the other's actions, his commitment to the other person will cause him to stand beside that individual. This can be seen in a mother's love for a wayward child, a spouse's love for an adulterous mate, or a child's love for an abusive parent.

A person who is committed does not let go easily when adverse situations arise. He or she holds on and refuses to walk away when things get tough.

Spiritually, Christ calls us to the same kind of commitment when we walk with Him. Difficulties and adverse circumstances will arise, but we must decide if Jesus is capable of overcoming all we face in life. If so, then we need to trust Him in every situation and give Him the freedom to use every circumstance in our lives to mold and refine us into a vessel of honor, sanctified and useful to the Master.

These words are easy to say but sometimes difficult to believe and obey, especially when problems arise. Our first response may be to reach out to anyone in listening range who is patient enough to hear our problem, or to rush into action to circumvent whatever is happening. Sometimes we may ask for prayer and wait for an answer. But rarely do we offer the situation to God, thank Him for what is happening, ask for His guidance, and pray that He be glorified, or honored, in the situation.

Why isn't the last option our first choice, especially since, knowing who Jesus is, we have committed our lives to Him? Could it be that we do not trust Him to overcome all obstacles and bring about a victorious end? Commitment without trust leads to a lopsided relationship.

## TRUST IS THE FOUNDATION

Isn't life good when things are going our way? It's even better when our emotions are touched while participating in a worship service. We can meditate on the words and nod in agreement, especially when we are emotionally satisfied.

But what happens when problems arise and answers cannot be found? What happens to our emotions? Are they as upbeat as before? Probably not. Is peace a reality in difficult situations? Usually not. Jesus says in John 14:27, "Peace I leave with you; my peace I give you, I do not give to you as the world gives. Do not let your hearts be troubled and do not be afraid."

If we believe Jesus' words and trust in Him, why should we expect our lives to be any different from His life on earth? Jesus encountered problems, but He trusted God the Father to carry Him through. Jesus knew that nothing on earth could overcome God the Father, therefore, His peace could not be shaken. Our trust determines the stability of our peace.

Webster defines trust as: "A confident reliance on the integrity, veracity, or justice of another; confidence; faith; also, the person or thing so trusted." How can we ask Jesus to be our Savior without trusting Him?

Isaiah 43:2 says, "When you pass through the waters, I will be with you; and when you pass through the rivers, they will not sweep over you. When you walk through the fire, you will not be burned; the flames will not set you ablaze."

That's the kind of trust we need if we have asked Jesus to be our Savior. We need to know in our hearts, minds, and spirits that Jesus will take us through all He allows in our lives—in His timing and in His way. When we come to this level of commitment and trust, then we are ready to make Jesus Lord of our lives. Only then are we ready to become a vessel that can be fully used by Him.

## JESUS AS LORD

When Jesus walked on earth, He asked His disciples who people said He was. Then He brought the question closer to home when He asked them who they (the disciples) said He was. Matthew 16:16 records Simon Peter's response: "You are the Christ, the Son of the living God."

If Jesus required the apostles to know who He is, would He require less of us today? Even though the apostles walked with Jesus during His three-year ministry on earth, it was not until after Jesus' resurrection that Thomas declared, "My Lord and My God!"

Each of us must decide if we will submit to the idea that Jesus is Lord of our lives during our time on earth. Accepting Jesus as Lord of our lives gives us freedom to accept whatever God the Father allows in our lives. We are then able to respond to all situations in a manner that brings honor and glory to God.

This is our ultimate goal. But most of us feel we are far from this goal. Be encouraged, because as long as we are on earth, God is giving us the opportunity to draw closer to Him.

## ARE YOU KNOWN BY JESUS?

Jesus does not force us to accept Him as Savior and Lord. See, for instance, His call of the first disciples in Matthew 4:18-22:

*As Jesus was walking beside the Sea of Galilee, he saw two brothers, Simon called Peter and his brother Andrew. They were casting a net into the lake, for they were fishermen. "Come, follow me," Jesus said, "and I will make you fishers of men." At once they left their nets and followed him. Going on from there, he saw two other brothers, James son of Zebedee and his brother John. They were in a boat with their father Zebedee, preparing their nets. Jesus called them, and immediately they left the boat and their father and followed him.*

Today, He simply speaks to us through His word, other believers, circumstances, and nature to direct our attention to Him. Just as He called His disciples, He also calls us.

Revelation 3:20 says, "Here I am! I stand at the door and knock. If anyone hears my voice and opens the door, I will come in and eat with him, and he with me." It is up to us to hear and receive Jesus, and invite Him into our lives. Unless we desire a relationship with Him, we will miss His call because knowing, loving, and serving Him are not priorities in our lives.

Association with those who have accepted Christ as Savior and Lord does not count because He knows those who are His. Attending church, Bible study, prayer groups, or religious activities are meaningless if a person has not accepted Jesus as Lord and Savior of his or her life.

Those who are known by Jesus are those who know who He is and their position before Him. They accept His death on the cross and resurrection from the dead as the payment for their sin. These people have humbled their hearts and try to put Him first in all things and try not to pursue selfish motives or desires. But we are all sinners, and we do not always do what we know to do.

Some may ask, "Isn't God a God of love? How can He pick and choose whom He will love? If He created all of us, why should He make a distinction between individuals?"

Without a doubt, God is a loving God. It is not His desire for any to perish. Second Peter 3:9 says, "[God] is patient with you, not wanting anyone to perish, but everyone to come to repentance."

Some believe we cannot come to God unless He has chosen us to come to Him. Others believe that we come into a relationship with God based on our decision to know Him. Both agree that Christ's death on the cross allows believers to have a restored relationship with God.

God knows our hearts. He knows who loves Him enough to willingly repent—turn from their lifestyle of self-centeredness—and humble themselves before Him. However, this does not mean that a person who repents and accepts Christ as Savior and Lord no longer sins. It means that, when such a person sins, he can confess his sin and be forgiven according to 1 John 1:8-10:

> *If we claim to be without sin, we deceive ourselves and the truth is not in us. If we confess our sins, he is faithful and just and will forgive us our sins and purify us from all unrighteousness. If we claim we have not sinned, we make him out to be a liar and his word has no place in our lives.*

Even though we may deceive ourselves because of self-denial or our refusal to see and acknowledge our sin, we do not deceive God. He intimately knows us and sees us as we are. Hebrews 4:12-13 says:

> *For the word of God is living and active. Sharper than any double-edged sword, it penetrates even to dividing soul and spirit, joints and marrow; it judges the thoughts and attitudes of the heart. Nothing in all creation is hidden from God's sight. Everything is uncovered and laid bare before the eyes of him to whom we must give account.*

Scripture is God's message to us. We can choose to accept or reject it. Ignorance of God's word is rejection of it. A person is either in darkness or in the light. 1 John 1:5-7 says:

> *This is the message we have heard from him and declare to you: God is light; in him there is no darkness at all. If we*

*claim to have fellowship with him yet walk in the darkness,*
*we lie and do not live by the truth. But if we walk in the light,*
*as he is in the light, we have fellowship with one another, and*
*the blood of Jesus, his Son, purifies us from all sin.*

We must determine if God knows us or not. If we choose to do as we please, deliberately disobeying or ignoring Scripture, God does not know us. When we choose to obey Scripture and submit our will to God by doing what pleases Him instead of ourselves, God knows us.

When we are known by God, the blood of Jesus cleanses us from all sin. We have unity with God as well as other believers when we walk in the light.

## PERSONAL APPLICATION

This chapter began with Wanda telling her friend Lisa that she did not feel close to God. To compensate for her "lack of closeness," Wanda thought that more activity would solve her problem. Lisa suggested that Wanda become more knowledgeable of the Bible, but Wanda felt she didn't have the time for such a commitment. When Lisa reminded her of the time she spent getting to know her husband before they were married, Wanda saw that as different. She did, however, acknowledge that time spent with her husband before marriage laid the foundation for the rest of their lives together.

Many people don't see their union with Jesus as a marital relationship, but John the Baptist did. When John's disciples questioned him about Jesus, he said in John 3:27-30:

*A man can receive only what is given him from heaven. You*
*yourselves can testify that I said, "I am not the Christ but*
*am sent ahead of him." The bride belongs to the bride-*
*groom. The friend who attends the bridegroom waits and*
*listens for him, and is full of joy when he hears the bride-*
*groom's voice. That joy is mine, and it is now complete. He*
*must become greater; I must become less.*

The same traits that determine whether a human relationship is successful or not—high levels of trust, commitment, respect, and personal knowledge of one another—are necessary in establishing and maintaining a relationship with Jesus. It's easy to admire a person from a distance because there is no emotional connection with that individual. But Jesus is not asking us to admire Him from a distance. He wants us to know Him personally and discover that He is all He claims to be.

How will we know He is the good shepherd as He claims in John 10:11 when He said—"I am the good shepherd. The good shepherd lays down his life for the sheep,"—if we have not experienced His goodness?

How can we trust Him when He says, "I have told you these things, so that in me you may have peace. In this world you will have trouble. But take heart! I have overcome the world!" (John 16:33)? It's hard to do this when life's problems are beating us to the ground in hopes of sucking our life's breath away. Can we turn to Him in complete confidence and choose to believe Him regardless of what's going on in our lives?

Our response during difficult times is an outcome of what we truly believe. When we are pressed from all sides, how we react comes from inside.

It's easy to pretend that we are in fellowship with Jesus when life is going smoothly because we can pick and choose how to respond in a situation. That is not the case when everything is falling apart. There isn't time to hide behind an emotional mask. What's inside of us comes tumbling out. A person is either committed to Christ and walking with Him or not. There's no middle ground.

We all experience hard times. Many of us have been treated unfairly. Some have experienced divorce or have been victimized in some other way. Some may have been subjected to physical or emotional abuse, while others have endured the loss of a loved one. How do we react? Perhaps we confide in a trusted friend all the storms that are taking place in our lives.

How much more should the burdens of our heart be shared with the One who "rebuked the wind and said to the waves, 'Quiet!

Be still!' Then the wind died down and it was completely calm" (Mark 4:39). Knowing the character of Jesus, as revealed in the Bible, will help us to decide whether He can be trusted and followed or not.

Is there anything too hard for God? That question can only be answered with certainty after we learn to trust Jesus. Entering into a two-way communication is the first step in building a relationship with Jesus. As with any significant person in our lives, agreeing to spend time with someone is the first step to getting to know the person.

Time spent together sharing—being in another's presence and valuing that person—helps the relationship to succeed. A great relationship does not develop overnight but over time. We should also expect our relationship with Jesus to get better and better over time.

In our opening story when Wanda asked, "What if I don't like how things are going? Who am I going to complain to?" she acknowledged a valid concern. People are different. But, as the saying goes: "opposites attract." It is not surprising that sinful man is attracted to a holy God.

Problems arise when a person's beliefs differ from God's word. As in any relationship, someone has to submit to the authority of the other if harmony is to be maintained.

In today's culture, the positive value of submission is not always recognized. Even so, submission is required in almost every aspect of our lives. Therefore, we must learn submission if we are to build our relationship with God.

# Chapter Two

# Clay Vessels:
# Hard to Distinguish
# from the World

*We have this treasure in jars of clay to show that this all-surpassing power is from God and not from us.*

2 Corinthians 4:7

Time for our annual guy trip! Drinking, new sights, and pleasure! What more could a person want?" asked Bob as he grinned and looked around at his partners.

"It doesn't get any better than that!" said Kevin. With the exception of Mike, the rest of the group nodded in agreement.

"I've been thinking about our trip, and I don't think I'm going this year. My church is having a men's retreat that weekend, and I'd like to go to that," said Mike.

"Are you crazy? You're choosing a church event over a good time? This isn't the Mike I know," said Bob. "Will the real Mike speak up?"

"Yeah, Mike, what's up with you?" asked Grant. "You've been acting a little strange lately. It seems that you aren't as interested in having fun with us as you once were."

Sam looked at Mike, squared his shoulders, and without smiling asked, "What do you mean you aren't going on our yearly trip? Do you think you're better than us?"

"No guys, you know I'm not like that. It's just that my church is having our men's retreat, and I want to attend because I've never gone before," said Mike. "All I know is that our '*it doesn't get any better than this*' trips leave me empty inside."

"What do you mean by empty? I'm not empty inside. You just need to know what you want, then go after it," said Kevin. "The challenge, chase, and conquering met your needs before. What's different now?"

"I can't verbalize the difference, but I know I've changed. It's not that I think I'm better than you, because I don't. We will always be friends, but I like what I'm learning at church. It's affecting how I think and act."

"You've always attended church. What's different now?" countered Kevin.

"I can't explain it to you. Just come and see for yourself. Then you'll understand why I enjoy going to church and want to learn more," said Mike.

"Are you telling us that you've changed and are no longer interested in all the things you did before?" questioned Grant.

"I'm not saying that exactly. I'm just saying I enjoy church and want to learn more about God."

"Why should we take you seriously when you're not serious? Man, you can't back up what you say. If you're so interested in God, why can't you tell us about Him? You never hesitated to tell us about any female who interested you. So why can't you tell us about your God?" asked Sam.

"It's because I don't know Him well enough. I know I'm different inside, but I can't tell you why. Is that so hard for you to understand? Why don't you just come to church with me and hear for yourselves? What are you afraid of?"

---

Although a successful, and normally articulate businessman, Mike cannot verbalize the spiritual changes that are taking place in his heart. He knows he is different because of his relationship with Jesus, but he doesn't know why. Maintaining former friendships is harder because his interests are changing.

Mike, like other new believers, must decide if his relationship with Jesus will replace his previous interests. If so, his journey to becoming a vessel of honor to God will probably lead him on a different path from his friends. As clay vessels we may look like the world, but our relationship with God is different from the world's.

## NO DISTINCTION FROM THE WORLD

When we are born, we are all alike. We inherit Adam and Eve's sin nature whether we like it or not. It has nothing to do with the choices we make, how good we are, how much money we have, or who we know. We all start life on the same spiritual level—as sinners. Socially, physically, and economically we may be different, but those distinctions apply to the world, not God.

It is hard for some to consider a newborn as a sinner because the child has done nothing, either good or bad, to warrant such a label. However, we find it easier to consider a person who chooses to indulge in whatever appeals to the flesh as a sinner. We say they have no discipline or restraint. But we are willing to wait until a child has had a sufficient amount of time to learn the difference between right and wrong, and are old enough to obey before making such a judgment on a newborn.

Waiting to label a newborn as a sinner, or not, does not take into consideration the sin nature that has been passed from Adam. Scripture says: "All have sinned and fall short of the glory of God" (Romans 3:23).

It is easy to call someone a sinner who continually does things not acceptable to us. But to lump all people, even newborns, into the sinner category when they haven't done anything we consider bad, is difficult. However, our method for judging is different from God's. He compares us to Himself. We fall short when measured against His standards because His standards of holiness are different from ours.

Psalm 14:2-3 says: "The Lord looks down from heaven on the sons of men to see if there are any who understand, any who seek God. All have turned aside, they have together become corrupt; there is no one who does good, not even one."

These words may appear harsh to some, especially those who do good works or live moral lives. We must remember that when

Adam and Even chose to go against God's will in Genesis 3, they were banished from the Garden of Eden. The loss of their innocence before God limited their access to and communion with Him. Therefore all who came after them also entered into this broken relationship with God.

The reason that all who follow Adam and Eve are not in communion with God is this: God created man in His own image according to Genesis 1:27. However, those who followed Adam were created in Adam's image according to Genesis 5:3. Adam reflected God's image, but his children reflected his image—fallen man.

Sometimes we may compare ourselves with others and think God likes us better because of our personalities. We must realize that our personalities do not determine our value to God. Rather, our personalities are examples of the creative genius of the One who formed us out of the dust of the ground. It shows how He took clay, molded it into His image to create man, and breathed into man's nostrils the breath of life.

Clay—made alive—in the image of its Creator. But when we are born, we are alive merely physically, and have not yet become alive spiritually. Only when we hear and respond to God's call through His Son, Jesus, are we on the path to becoming a vessel of honor, sanctified and useful to the Master. No longer will we be on the same footing as the world. And no longer will the world have the same influence or control over us, unless we choose to submit to the things that entice us.

## Faith in God, not Self or Others

Responding to God's call does not mean everyone should bow to us and accept whatever we say. That would surely ignite the unquenchable flames of pride and quickly lead to our downfall. Rather, it opens the door that was once closed to us as we begin our journey to becoming like Jesus. Very few of us master anything the first time we try it. It is no different with our walk with Christ.

Regardless of the number of years it has taken to bring us into a relationship with God through Jesus, we all have baggage from our previous way of life. In order to get to where we are now, we have had to depend on someone or something—the object of our faith.

One of the first issues we will have to deal with, if our faith is to be redirected and placed in God, will be to put whoever or whatever we called upon, or whoever we trusted to come to our aid in times of distress, in line behind God. Hebrews 12:2 says, "Let us fix our eyes on Jesus, the author and perfecter of our faith."

No one likes being displaced. Some parents may challenge their children's belief in Jesus if the focus is no longer on accepted family traditions and values. This can happen in Christian as well as non-Christian families.

Some Christian parents may disagree with their children's decision to walk with Christ, if it involves an area in which the parents have not fully surrendered to Christ. This could include missionary work in poor areas of this country or another country. It may also include a child's willing acceptance of a less than prosperous lifestyle.

Some may also object to what they perceive as a radical change in their child, especially if it involves a passion for Christ that convicts the parent's lukewarm faith. These children reject the belief that Christ is good as long as believing in Him leads to a life of blessing. They willingly seek God's kingdom and His righteousness first.

Those who are faced with a decision to maintain their belief in Jesus over the objections of parents who have faithfully supported, loved, and cared for them over the years, struggle emotionally. But when that decision is made, their faith rests firmly in God and not man, even though, being imperfect (as we all are), they may stumble along the way.

If parents are not a hurdle for us, peer rejection may be. Some of us may know that our parents will always be there for us, so we are not afraid to put our trust in Jesus. However, friends may not be as totally devoted as some parents. As long as we are in step with them, and in agreement with their actions and beliefs, we can count on their loyalty and support. When they perceive us as different, and not going along with the program as we once did, they assume something is wrong with us—not them.

If friends feel we are not a threat to them—their beliefs or actions—they will maintain their friendship with us. But if they feel our new way of thinking condemns them, even though we never say a word, they will be too busy to return our calls or spend time with us. Their fear of us rejecting them leads them to reject us. If we are not secure in our faith in Jesus, we will be tempted to value our friends over our relationship with Him.

Instead of allowing rejection to deflate us and cause us to grieve the loss of our friends or a lifestyle that was unfulfilling, we should take this opportunity to develop our relationship with Christ and others who are in Him. The more we learn of Him, the more we can become like Him. Once our faith is strengthened and our walk secure, we can then return to our friends and share our beliefs in a way that does not threaten them. Our love for our friends deepens our desire to share what's different about us, but we must never force our beliefs on them. They should have the freedom to respond to God's call in their lives, just as we did.

True faith should be in God, not self or others.

## WAVERING IN OUR WALK

If we are to be vessels of honor, sanctified and useful to the Master, sooner or later there must be a distinction between us and the world. When God calls us, we are usually in full step with everyone around us. What our friends like, so do we, even if we know our actions are not pleasing to God.

As with any newborn, we are mostly focused on self. Our needs and our desires are what matters most. If we continue to allow ourselves to be our main concern, we are putting ourselves in God's place. The transition to putting God first is not always immediate or final. As with other stages in our lives, it's a growth process. Sometimes we are successful, and sometimes we're not.

No one expects a baby to walk, talk, or behave like an adult. Neither should we expect new believers to act like those who have walked with Christ for years. But neither should we encourage or allow new believers to have any other standard but the one set by Christ. Know that believers, new or maturing, will not always obey God's Word. That is why we are told to ask God to forgive our sins. However, our lapses into sin should become fewer and fewer as we walk with Christ because we seek to please God, not ourselves. The things that once held us in bondage should no longer have such a stronghold in our lives. Gradually, we are able to obtain victory in those areas. We should not be easily led astray by food, drugs, alcohol, sex, or self-centeredness.

Until we decide to seek first God's kingdom and righteousness, we will waver in our walk with Him because we are still trying to hold onto the things of the world. Scripture says we cannot serve two masters. We must choose to whom we will give our allegiance. It will either be the world or God, not both. Before we make that final decision, we will try our best to come up with an acceptable combination of God and the world.

Because we are in the world, that's what we see and believe. Even though we have accepted Jesus, our spiritual vision is not twenty/twenty. Therefore, we fail to see the harm of mixing a holy God with an unholy world. The things we call good are not necessarily what God calls good. Until we are in sync with God and wholeheartedly agree with what He calls good, we will waver in our walk with Him because of disobedience. This can happen at any stage in our walk with God—clay, wood, silver, or gold. Any disobedience is disobedience and interrupts our walk with God.

## CHOOSING TO OBEY GOD

Most of us rejoice when we decide to follow Jesus. We rush to tell others, expecting them to rejoice with us. However, that is not always the case. People's attitudes do not change because we change. If they know and love Jesus, they will be happy for us and encourage our spiritual growth. If they do not know or love Him, they may accept our decision, without supporting it, or they may question our decision. Regardless of others' response to our decision to follow Jesus, we must honor our commitment and choose to obey Jesus' call on our lives.

A toddler's world consists of all that is familiar to him, and as far as he is concerned, nothing is important outside his sphere of influence. It is the parent's responsibility to train the toddler so that he learns to respond in an acceptable manner. Even though the toddler does not realize it, his actions affect others as well as himself. New believers are like toddlers. They must learn to obey God's Word instead of pleasing themselves.

At times it is difficult for those beginning their walk with Jesus to turn their backs on all that is familiar to them—having fun, setting and achieving personal goals, perfecting self, or just relaxing and doing whatever comes natural. They prefer what they are familiar with, just as a baby initially prefers a bottle over a cup. When a toddler transitions from a bottle to a cup, he no longer desires a bottle. He realizes that what he now has is just as satisfying.

New believers may feel they will miss something and may not take their commitment to Jesus seriously. Although they aren't doing what they once did, their lives aren't exactly in alignment with God's Word. Many teens and young adults fall into this category. Their desire to enjoy life while they are young, reserving their obedience to God for when they are older, causes many to stumble and fall. It is hard for them to understand that obeying Jesus and walking with Him is fun and enjoyable, not boring and pleasureless.

Some students in a high school Sunday school class said they would live a life dedicated to God when they got older. When asked how they knew they would live that long or how they knew they could turn from a lifestyle of sin, they could not answer. For the moment, their desire was to be like their peers. They could not envision a fulfilling relationship with Jesus.

Instead of thinking that life as they know it will last forever, new believers need to ask God to change their perspective and see their lives in relation to eternity. They should no longer live for the moment, pursuing pleasure and meaning. Even Solomon, with all his riches and the ability to do whatever he desired, discovered that "everything was meaningless, a chasing after the wind; nothing was gained under the sun" (Ecclesiastes 2:11).

To further strengthen his point, Solomon closes the book of Ecclesiastes with these words: "Here is the conclusion of the matter: 'Fear God and keep his commandments, for this is the whole duty of man. For God will bring every deed into judgment, including every hidden thing, whether it is good or evil.'"

We may disagree with Solomon, but know that God appeared to Solomon in a dream and told him to ask for whatever he wanted. Solomon acknowledged that he was only a child and didn't know how to lead Israel. Therefore, he asked for a discerning heart so he could rule the people and know the difference between right and wrong.

God's response to Solomon's request is found in 1 Kings 3:11-15:

> Since you have asked for this and not for long life or wealth
> for yourself, nor have asked for the death of your enemies
> but for discernment in administering justice, I will give you
> a wise and discerning heart, so that there will never have
> been anyone like you, nor will there ever be. Moreover, I will
> give you what you have not asked for—both riches and
> honor—so that in your lifetime you will have no equal
> among kings. And if you walk in my ways and obey my
> statues and commands as David your father did, I will give
> you a long life.

Not only should new believers not be afraid to leave their former way of life, but they should also realize they are not able to obey God without His help. Solomon acknowledged his inability to lead Israel. He relied on God and depended on Him to help him accomplish the work entrusted to him. God provided all Solomon needed. As God helped Solomon, He will also help all those who recognize their weakness and call on Him.

The Apostle Paul also delighted in weaknesses, hardships, insults, persecutions and difficulties, for he learned that when he was weak, God made him strong. God's words to Paul concerning his weakness are found in 2 Corinthians 12:9: "My grace is sufficient for you, for my power is made perfect in weakness." As God promised to help Paul, He will help all those who depend on Him.

Those who choose to obey God's Word can depend on His help in times of need. God is faithful and will not allow His children to be overcome by the world.

## SANCTIFIED CLAY VESSEL

Sanctification happens when we conscientiously choose to obey God and be separated for Him. *Vine's Complete Expository Dictionary of Old and New Testament Words* says: "Holy character is not vicarious, i.e., it cannot be transferred or imputed, it is an individual possession, built up, little by little, as the result of obedience to the Word of God, and of following the example of Christ."

When we respond to God's call to us by inviting Jesus into our hearts, we have begun our journey of sanctification, even though outwardly we are no different from those around us. Once we receive Christ, we are alive spiritually. Our second birth opens our minds, eyes, ears, and hearts to what we could not understand or perceive before.

Ephesians 4:22-24 says:

*You were taught, with regard to your former way of life, to put off your old self, which is being corrupted by its deceitful desire; to be made new in the attitude of your minds; and to put on the new self, created to be like God in true righteousness and holiness.*

Our desire is to please God instead of ourselves. We are able to choose to behave in a way that honors our new beliefs. We are empowered by our new nature to turn away from things that dishonor God and His gospel.

We may feel that others should see and understand the inner changes that are occurring in us. They may recognize that something is different about us, but they probably will not know or understand the difference. Just as we could not discern spiritually before our salvation, neither can they. Men who have had only physical births, not spiritual births, can only grasp that which can be seen by the physical eye.

Vine's explanation of sanctification continues:

*Since every believer is sanctified in Christ Jesus, a common New Testament designation of all believers is 'saints,' i.e., 'sanctified' or 'holy ones.' Thus sainthood, or sanctification, is not an attainment, it is the state into which God, in grace, calls sinful men, and in which they begin their course as Christians.*

New believers, even though they are clay vessels, are valuable to God. Being able to describe their relationship with God to others is not as important as the decision they have made to walk with God.

The man born blind that was healed by Jesus did not have much knowledge about Him. But when questioned by the Pharisees about his healing, he responded, "One thing I do know. I was blind but now I see!"

New believers are only responsible for sharing what they know—their personal testimony. No one can argue with that. As they grow in their relationship with God and walk with Him in obedience, they will be able to share His Word in a manner others can understand.

## PERSONAL APPLICATION

"It doesn't get any better than this," is a phrase that is often used by the world to ignite our passions, desires, or lusts. Things outside of us cannot fill the emptiness within us—no matter how much fun we have, how many things we accumulate, or how much money we have. The world's salve cannot heal our spiritual void.

Mike, like other new believers, knew he had changed inside. Defining that change to his friends was difficult. Jesus understood that, because when two of John's disciples followed Him, He invited them to come and find out for themselves who He was. Andrew, one of the two who accepted Jesus' invitation, believed Jesus was the Messiah after spending the day with Him. He found his brother, Simon Peter, told him about Jesus, and then took him to meet Jesus.

Jesus found Philip and told him to follow Him. After listening to Jesus, Philip found Nathanael and told him about Jesus. Nathanael doubted that anything good could come from Nazareth, Jesus' home town. Philip never argued with him, he simply said, "Come and see" (John 1:46).

The Samaritan woman, after her encounter with Jesus at the well, ran back to her village and told the people, "Come, see a man who told me everything I ever did. Could this be the Christ?" (John 4:29). She did not tell them about the living water Jesus offered her or His claim to be Messiah. She simply invited them to come hear Him. She allowed them the opportunity to make their own decision regarding whether He was the Savior of the world.

As sanctified vessels, we may not know much about Jesus when we begin our walk with Him. That puts us in good company, because the disciples weren't very knowledgeable either when they met Jesus. Yet, every true believer is compelled to tell others about Jesus because it's hard not to share good things that happen to us.

Those who are unwilling to share Jesus or their salvation story, with friends, family, or associates should evaluate their commitment to Christ. People indwelt by the Holy Spirit have changed lives. Those who say they are believers, yet cling to their former lifestyles walk in darkness. It is fruitless to have light and conceal it.

Matthew 5:14-16 says:

*You are the light of the world. A city on a hill cannot be hidden. Neither do people light a lamp and put it under a bowl. Instead they put it on its stand, and it gives light to everyone in the house. In the same way, let your light shine before men, that they may see your good deeds and praise your Father in heaven.*

Those who say, "It doesn't get any better than this," have only experienced what the world has to offer and have not tasted the goodness of God. They enjoy the rain, the sun, the breath of life, and other general goodness that God freely gives to all men, but they have not come into a personal knowledge of Him. They are bound by the fleeting pleasures of sin. Neither are their feet on solid rock because spiritually they dwell in a pit, surrounded by miry clay.

Moses enjoyed all the pleasures Egypt had to offer. When he attempted to bring about what he felt was God's will for Israel, he ended up killing a man. To his surprise, some Israelites had witnessed the murder and therefore did not respect his authority. Fearing for his life, he fled to Midian. Although he was accepted by the Midianites, and even married one, the emptiness he felt inside can be seen in the name he gave his son, Gershom—an alien in a foreign land. It was not until he responded to God's call from the burning bush that his life began to change.

Yet, God's call to Moses did not instantly turn his life around. The first words out of Moses' mouth when he learned that God wanted to send him to Egypt were: "Who am I that I should go to Pharaoh and bring the Israelites out of Egypt?" (Exodus 3:11). Moses did not know God or His power. In fact, he had an excuse for everything God told him to do. We don't know God or His power when we enter into a relationship with Him, but that should not keep us from telling others about Him or speaking the words He gives us.

Only as we grow in our relationship with God, do we begin to realize that knowing, loving, and serving God is much better than anything the world has to offer. Our family, friends, and associates will notice a change in our lives. We should not be surprised when they ask what has made a difference in us. They have walked with us and know the true us, if we have been transparent in our relationship with them. They know whether we have changed or not. They can tell from our actions whether our change is genuine.

We cannot continue to do the same old things and expect to be a witness of the goodness of God to others. The world has a label for those who attempt to live such a life—hypocrite. It's not our knowledge of God that determines our value to Him, but our decision to give our hearts and lives to Him. That's what makes us sanctified, a vessel of honor, useful to the Master.

# CHAPTER THREE

# Don't Give Up!

## Perseverance

Rachel, a single mother with three children, sat at her kitchen table in the predawn hours one Sunday morning. Just when things had seemed to be going well for her, the van driver for her car pool had driven off before she had finished exiting the van. The right side of her body had been injured and she did not know when she could return to work. Frustrated, she sighed, rested her left elbow on the table, and cupped her chin. As tears came to her eyes, she prayed:

> "Lord, I'm tired. Whenever I overcome in one area, You test me in another. I need a break! Haven't I shown myself faithful? Did I find solace in another man when my husband chose to be unfaithful? No. His arrogant attitude and belittling remarks almost made me doubt my worth. Without You in my life, I would have believed every word he said. After all, who knew me more intimately than he did? Why would I have doubted the one I promised to be united to until death parted us? Yet You allowed Hubert to do as he

*pleased, without any regard for me or our children. He said he didn't want to be married anymore and walked out. Where is the fairness in that? He knows the needs of the family, yet he's delinquent with the support checks and doesn't see or relate to the children as he should.*

*Lord, You know the problems don't stop there. I work harder than anyone at my job, not because I want to, but because I have to. Who will provide for my children if not me? Yet all my hard work has not paid off on the job. Others get promoted but not me. Why? If I'm good enough to train those promoted, why can't I have the job? You know my family needs the money. Everything's going up except my take-home pay. Why should my children and I be penalized because of my company's decision to eliminate some of our insurance benefits? It doesn't stop there. Look at the price of gasoline. Every increase forces me to make a sacrifice some-where else. Lord, You know the desire of my heart has been to move to a better home. How can I do that when housing costs are astronomical?*

*Lord, You said to put You first, and everything else would fall into place. I am putting You first, but nothing is falling into place. Are You there? Am I not understanding Your promises? What should I do that I'm not already doing? Lord, are You listening to me?*

*Lord, what about the good things I do? Not only do I attend church, but I also take my children so they can learn about You. I monitor the television programs they watch, their time on the computer, the music they listen to, and the friends they hang out with. Do You know how unpopular I am when I refuse to allow my children to imitate what they see or hear in today's culture? There are even some in the church who disagree with how I raise my children. I've heard some of the things they have said about me behind my back. What kind of example are they to my children? Yet they are the ones who seem to prosper, not me.*

*Lord, I know You are in control of all things, and I know You won't allow anything in my life that I can't handle. But Lord, I'm getting tired. Can You show me just a little light to keep me going? I need to know You're there, and that You have the best interests of my children and me at heart. Lord, I'm not asking for much, just a little something to give me the incentive to continue trusting You no matter what comes my way.*

---

## The Purpose of Trials

Webster defines trial as, "the action or process of trying or putting to the proof; a test of faith, patience, or stamina through subjection to suffering or temptation; *broadly* : a source of vexation or annoyance." But knowing the definition and successfully passing through a trial may be two different things.

It is easy to claim victory in an area. Just ask any elementary school student who claims to have studied, yet fails the test. A word may be spelled differently than it sounds. True knowledge of the correct spelling of a word allows a student to spell it correctly in any situation. The same is true when a person who claims to have faith is tested. If a person's faith is genuine, the person will have victory regardless of the circumstances.

In the book of Daniel, the faith of Daniel, Hananiah, Mishael, and Azariah remained the same when their names changed to Belteshazzar, Shadrach, Meshach, and Abednego. Outward circumstances did not dictate their personal beliefs. The four Hebrew young men knew the God they served, and they trusted Him to meet their needs when they made a request to eat vegetables and drink water instead of eating the royal food and drinking wine from the king's table. Even though God honored their request and made them healthier and better nourished than the others, that was not the end of their trials.

King Nebuchadnezzar had a troubling dream and refused to tell the astrologers, magicians, enchanters, sorcerers, and wise men what he had dreamed. Yet, the king demanded that these people interpret his dream or they would be cut into pieces and their houses would be turned into piles of rubble. When Daniel heard about the king's plan, he went to Hananiah, Mishael, and Azariah and asked them to plead for God's favor and revelation of the mystery so their lives would be saved. They, along with the others, would also be destroyed if they failed the king. Again, God answered and gave Daniel the interpretation of the dream.

The reprieve did not last long for Hananiah, Mishael, and Azariah. Soon their refusal to bow down to the golden image of King Nebuchadnezzar infuriated the king, as did their conversation with him—Daniel 3:16-18:

> O Nebuchadnezzar, we do not need to defend ourselves
> before you in this matter. If we are thrown into the blazing
> furnace, the God we serve is able to save us from it, and he
> will rescue us from your hand, O king. But even if he does
> not, we want you to know, O king, that we will not serve
> your gods or worship the image of gold you have set up.

The king was so angry with them that he ordered the fire to be heated seven times hotter and for his strongest soldiers to throw them in. The flames killed the soldiers but not Hananiah, Mishael, and Azariah.

God promises in Isaiah 43:2, "When you walk through the fire, you will not be burned; the flames will not set you ablaze." We cannot accept and believe these words in the midst of fiery trials if our previous trials have not laid the foundation for such trust and faith in God. Reliance on self or others does not lead to faith in God or trust in His Word. Our faith is not developed by telling God how to act or what to do in a situation, but, as Hananiah, Mishael, and Azariah did, in trusting God even when we don't know the outcome.

Later, God gave King Nebuchadnezzar a dream concerning His plan to humble him. Of course, the king did not understand the dream because few people see themselves as they really are. However,

God allowed Daniel to interpret the dream for Nebuchadnezzar. When the dream was fulfilled, the king honored God, not Daniel.

A person would probably think that the king's son should have learned from all that happened to his father, but that was not the case. Nebuchadnezzar's son, Belshazzar, only relied on Daniel as a last resort. After he and his guests drank from the golden goblets that had been taken from the temple in Jerusalem, a hand appeared and wrote on the wall. The king's face turned pale, his knees knocked together, and his legs gave way. Daniel was the only one who could read and interpret the writing for the king. Unfortunately, the interpretation foretold the king's death as well as his successor—King Darius, ruler of the Medes and Persians.

Daniel, Hananiah, Mishael, and Azariah had spent many years under King Nebuchadnezzar and his son, yet they had to start from scratch under the new king. It's the same for believers today. What we did yesterday does not count. Each day is a new opportunity for us to stand firm and do what is right, regardless of the consequences. Since God is the same yesterday, today, and tomorrow, He can be counted on to meet the needs of His children, now, as in Daniel's day.

Trials cut away the chaff that has nothing to do with our faith in God or the truth of His Word. If we look to God and trust Him to intercede on our behalf in the way He chooses, then when God answers, our faith grows stronger. Increasing faith fuels our hope when we walk with God. Even in a fiery trial, our faith perseveres.

If Daniel had not trusted God when he refused to eat food from the king's table, how could he have trusted Him when thrown in the lion's den? Faith, like everything else, must be nurtured. Trials measure our depth of faith in God. For seventy years, God's people remained in captivity in Babylon. Daniel, Hananiah, Mishael, and Azariah persevered despite their circumstances. False accusations and the threat of death did not overcome their faith, but refined it. We, too, regardless of our situation, should trust God, pray for His mercy, trust Him with the outcome, and give Him the glory.

## Weariness in Doing Right When Powered by Self

Success energizes. Defeat cripples. Waiting deflates. Success encourages us to continue pursuing our goals. Defeat can discourage us and make us doubt the validity of accomplishing our goals. Waiting, especially over a long period of time, forces us to rethink and reevaluate our beliefs. If we do not guard our thought life, and remain hopeful while persevering in difficult circumstances, weariness will darken our vision and steal our joy. It is only human to become tired in battle, but we need to keep our eyes on the goal and strive to accomplish it.

Genesis 37–50 tells the story of Joseph and his family. God gave the young Joseph two dreams that foretold his future exaltation and his brothers' submission to him. However, the dreams did not tell how God intended to accomplish this goal in Joseph's life. Dreams of success energized Joseph. He did not hesitate to share his dreams with his brothers. Instead of rejoicing when hearing Joseph's dreams, his brothers despised him.

Like Joseph, many people share their good news with the expectation that others will be excited for them, only to discover that is not the case. As difficult as it may be, we must learn to keep some things to ourselves, especially if we are not sensitive as to how others may respond. Our good news may be for us alone—not others.

What's important is whether we choose to cling to and pursue God's Word, or believe the words of others and abandon God's plan for our lives. Perseverance, continuing in spite of difficulties, leads to success when we are weary.

Webster defines weary as: "Worn with exertion, vexation, or suffering; tired; fatigued. Discontented or vexed by continued endurance, or by something disagreeable." Ordinary problems in life can be irritating. Mental stress increases when suffering is the only outcome of doing right. Our faith determines whether we will remain steadfast or turn aside when facing difficulties.

Jacob, Joseph's father, sent him to check on his brothers. When he reached them, they took his ornamental coat, threw him in a cistern, and later sold him into slavery. Although Joseph cried out for help, his brothers refused to come to his aid. To cover their offense, the brothers slaughtered a goat, dipped Joseph's coat in its blood, and took it to their father, who assumed Joseph had been killed by an animal. Jacob's sons allowed him to grieve for his beloved child. None stepped forward to comfort him with the truth.

Is it any surprise that often others stand idly by when watching an innocent person suffer? Yet many believe that people are inherently good and will stand up for righteousness. Why? What evidence is there to support the inherent goodness of people? A blood tie to someone does not guarantee they will do the right thing. Neither does a spiritual connection with others, especially if their belief system is not grounded in God's Word.

Although Joseph was a slave in Egypt, God prospered him and gave him favor in his master Potiphar's eyes. Potiphar did not concern himself with anything because God blessed all Joseph did. However Joseph's faithfulness to Potiphar did not prevent Potiphar's wife from trying to seduce him. When he did not respond to her in the way she desired, she accused him of rape. God's blessings on Potiphar's household and Joseph's faithfulness to him did not reverse or erase the false accusations against Joseph. The charges stood and Joseph was thrown in prison.

Are there people today who have been falsely accused because they did not comply with the personal desires of another? How should they react? Should they pout and resent those whom they have faithfully served for not supporting them? Can they say for certain that this is not the plan God has chosen to use to bring about His greater purpose in their lives?

Bitterness and resentment are stumbling blocks we must overcome in the trials God allows in our lives. Joseph had to endure this trial and learn from it in order to accomplish God's purpose for his life. God allowed this training in humility so that later, when He lifted Joseph to power, Joseph would know whom it was he served, and why he was in a certain position. God exalted Joseph. He is also the one who will exalt us if we remain faithful to Him.

While in prison, Joseph interpreted the dreams of two of the king's servants—the cupbearer and the baker. The cupbearer promised that he would mention Joseph and his plight to Pharaoh when restored to his former position. That did not happen. Not until Pharaoh had a dream that the magicians and wise men could not interpret did the cupbearer remember Joseph and tell Pharaoh about him. Joseph's interpretation of the dream, and his plan for solving the problem, gave him favor in Pharaoh's eyes. He became second in command to Pharaoh and in charge of all Egypt.

At this point in Joseph's life, Scripture does not say whether he realized that God was weaving every situation in his life to accomplish His purpose for him. However, Scripture does show Joseph's faithfulness to God regardless of his circumstances. He did not swerve to the right or left when trusting God. We should imitate Joseph's faithfulness and trust in God regardless of where we are in our spiritual walk. Everyone has great hindsight, but God is more interested in our moment-by-moment dependence on Him.

These events took place over a long period in Joseph's life. He continued to persevere and remain faithful despite the mistreatment he received. It does not appear that he became weary in doing right because he never gave up hope of vindication. He looked for help from those around him but did not receive it. His dreams and his life were 180 degrees apart. Yet, he chose to trust God and await His timing. Are we willing to make that choice?

In Genesis 42, God fulfilled Joseph's first dream when his brothers came to Egypt to buy food. Not recognizing their brother, they bowed in submission because of his obviously high rank. When Joseph later revealed himself to his brothers, they were terrified because they knew how they had mistreated him. Yet, Joseph did not hold a grudge. He rejoiced at the anticipated reunion with his father and younger brother, Benjamin.

At last Jacob, renamed Israel by God, was comforted when he saw Joseph, his son, and said, "Now I am ready to die, since I have seen for myself that you are still alive" (Genesis 46:30). Jacob and his sons benefitted from God's blessings to Joseph. They also witnessed the fulfillment of Joseph's dream.

The young Joseph, who received God's dreams, differed from the older Joseph who realized those dreams. Young Joseph's faith and trust in God sustained him as he matured into an older, wiser Joseph who responded to his brothers in a godly manner regarding their mistreatment of him. In Genesis 50:19-21 Joseph says:

> *'Don't be afraid. Am I in the place of God? You intended to harm me, but God intended it for good to accomplish what is now being done, the saving of many lives. So then, don't be afraid. I will provide for you and your children.' And he reassured them and spoke kindly to them.*

How does Joseph's attitude compare to ours? How do we react toward others who have mistreated us?

It is not unfathomable to us that God may allow us to know His general plan for our lives. How many people have missed experiencing the fulfillment of God's plan because they did not persevere and endure the circumstances needed to refine and deepen their trust and faith in Him? Or how many have run ahead of God to accomplish His plan according to their understanding? No one likes suffering, but suffering has a purpose when it is in the will of God for a person's life. Unless we choose to persevere and endure all that comes our way with a godly attitude, we will not gain all God intended for us in allowing the suffering.

Growth is not static. Our faith must be stretched if God's grace is to be evident in our lives. Remaining the same as when He first calls us is not acceptable because He wants us to continually get to know Him better. Often, our flaws can only be removed through the tests and trials in our lives.

We may be very excited when we think God will use us greatly. Sometimes we may wonder why others do not see or understand God's call on our lives, but that should not discourage us. As we wait for God to use us, our initial excitement may dwindle. The longer we wait, the more we may begin to doubt. John the Baptist is a prime example.

Before John was conceived, an angel appeared to his father, Zechariah, as he ministered in the temple and told him of the great work John would do. Even in his mother's womb, John leaped at the sound of the pregnant virgin Mary. From birth, God the Holy Spirit indwelt John (Luke 1:13-15). When John baptized Jesus, God the Father spoke to him from heaven, confirming that Jesus is His Son.

As the angel had prophesied, John had a great ministry to the people of Israel. He turned the hearts of many Israelites back to their God, and he did not hesitate to stand against the wicked. However, near the end of his ministry, John sent his disciples to Jesus to ask, "Are you the one who was to come, or should we expect someone else?" (Matthew 11:3). John, filled with the Spirit, doubted, even though God had spoken to him. So we should not be surprised when we doubt because things do not turn out as we expected.

In response to John's question, Jesus said:

*Go back and report to John what you hear and see: The blind receive sight, the lame walk, those who have leprosy are cured, the deaf hear, the dead are raised, and the good news is preached to the poor. Blessed is the man who does not fall away on account of me (Matthew 11:4-6).*

Jesus' words were meant to encourage John. He also speaks encouraging words to us through Scripture. We must choose to read and believe His Word so we are strengthened and not discouraged when difficulties arise.

Jesus knew and acknowledged John the Baptist's worth before God. In Matthew 11:11, He said, "I tell you the truth: Among those born of women there has not risen anyone greater than John the Baptist; yet he who is least in the kingdom of heaven is greater than he." John was a vessel greatly used by God. He loved God and did all he could to further His kingdom. Yet, it seemed that his work had no impact.

Even though John got weary, he persevered until the end. He believed God and continued to work for Him. Should we do less, especially when considering Jesus' promise to give rest to the weary and burdened? We should persevere and endure because God does not give us more than we are able to bear.

## HOPE KINDLES PERSEVERANCE

*Vine's Complete Expository Dictionary of Old and New Testament Words* says "hope has to do with the unseen and the future and describes the happy anticipation of good."

A small group of believers meets weekly in Washington, D.C. at 7:00 A.M. to pray. Frank, the son of a Kansas farmer, told the group of his father's response to approaching storms. His father could see the storm from a distance, yet there was nothing he could do to prevent it from ravaging his fields. No amount of preparation or planning could prevent the weather patterns that birthed the June and July storms.

God knew the financial security of Frank's family depended on the crops in the fields, yet He allowed the storms. Should his father, Tom, have walked away from the land and chosen a different occupation? No. Tom, like other farmers, realized that God, not he, is in control. Therefore, he could weather the storms with a humble attitude and graciously continue the work God placed on his heart.

James 2:17-18 says, "In the same way, faith by itself, if it is not accompanied by action, is dead. But someone will say, 'You have faith; I have deeds.' Show me your faith without deeds, and I will show you my faith by what I do."

Tom's faith gave him the incentive to persevere despite storms and their impact upon his financial security. He genuinely believed that God would not allow more than he could handle in his life. How could he reject or despise the One who graciously met all his needs and the needs of his family? He had a job to do and occasional storms would not deter him from completing his work.

Tom's attitude toward God planted a seed of faith in Frank's life. Although Frank did not say whether his father faced the trials with joy, he recalled how his father persevered after the storm—full of hope, not overcome by circumstances.

James 1:3-4 says, "You know that the testing of your faith develops perseverance. Perseverance must finish its work so that you may be mature and complete, not lacking anything."

Tom never doubted God's goodness to him or his family. When we trust in God, we need to have the hope and perseverance of the farmer during the stormy seasons of life. Recognizing our helplessness in a situation should lead to our dependence and trust in God. Instead of looking to ourselves for the power to overcome or endure, we should look to God and trust in His goodness to bring us through whatever He allows in our lives.

We have freedom in Christ because He has broken sin's hold on our lives. Therefore, we are not like incarcerated prisoners who cannot make decisions regarding their circumstances. We should appreciate our freedom of choice, willingly submit to God, and humble ourselves before Him.

After listening to Frank's story of his father's faith, Fred, an older member of the group, remarked that Americans appear to have less faith today than when the majority of the population farmed. He surmised that as people moved into the cities they had the illusion that they were less dependent on God and more dependent on themselves.

Rebecca, a younger member of the group, sang a song that compared God to silver, gold, and diamonds. She said that if people really believed that God is more precious than anything they desire, then their perspective toward Him would be different. They would know, love, serve, and value Him.

When people realize their helplessness and lack of power to change a situation, that's when they are ready to trust God and submit to His sovereignty. Hope grounded in God, not self, leads to perseverance regardless of circumstances.

If we seek to control situations, devastating events may cause us to become depressed, overwhelmed, or lack the desire to persevere. However powerful we may consider ourselves to be, we cannot victoriously overcome every situation we encounter.

Proverbs 30:4 lays a great foundation for a humble spirit and a hopeful heart. It says, "Who has gone up to heaven and come down? Who has gathered up the wind in the hollow of his hands? Who has wrapped up the waters in his cloak? Who has established all the ends of the earth?"

If we acknowledge our helplessness and rely on God, we have the desire and spiritual incentive to persevere because we know that greater is He who is in us than he who is in the world (1 John 4:4).

## PERSONAL APPLICATION

At the beginning of Chapter 3, Rachel's prayer shows her love for God, but it also reveals her doubts concerning His faithfulness in meeting her needs. God created us and knows us, therefore, when we are transparent in our prayers, He is pleased because we are admitting what He already knows we feel. Rachel could have prayed Psalm 17:1-9:

> *Hear, O Lord, my righteous plea; listen to my cry. Give ear to my prayer—it does not rise from deceitful lips. May my vindication come from You; may your eyes see what is right. Though you probe my heart and examine me at night, though you test me, you will find nothing; I have resolved that my mouth will not sin. As for the deeds of men—by the word of your lips I have kept myself from the ways of the violent. My steps have held to your paths; my feet have not slipped. I call on you, O God, for you will answer me; give ear to me and hear my prayer. Show the wonder of your great love, you who save by your right hand those who take refuge in you from their foes. Keep me as the apple of your eye; hide me in the shadow of your wings from the wicked who assail me, from my mortal enemies who surround me.*

The Psalms are full of hearts being exposed to God in prayer. When threatened and pursued by Saul, David fled. Yet he never ceased praying to God or relying on Him to bring about a favorable outcome regarding his situation. David's faith in God fueled his hope to persevere, regardless of the circumstances he faced. We should never be afraid to cry out to God in prayer. He is the same yesterday, today, and tomorrow. He heard and answered the prayers of His servants before us and He will continue to answer the prayers of all who call upon Him. Psalm 121 reads:

*I lift up my eyes to the hills—where does my help come from? My help comes from the Lord, the Maker of heaven and earth. He will not let your foot slip—he who watches over you will not slumber; indeed, he who watches over Israel will neither slumber nor sleep. The Lord watches over you—the Lord is your shade at your right hand; the sun will not harm you by day, nor the moon by night. The Lord will keep you from all harm—he will watch over your life; the Lord will watch over your coming and going both now and forevermore.*

When we accept and believe what we read in Scripture, our seed of hope should grow, overcoming every area of doubt in our heart. We should not expect an easy life because Jesus did not have an easy life. If it is our desire for others to see Him in us, then we should persevere and refuse to turn from following and obeying God all our days on earth so that we may honor and glorify Him.

Rachel has the right spirit because she made her requests known to God instead of complaining to others or sulking in silence. When we sincerely feel that we cannot go on, God is faithful. He will not allow us to be tempted beyond what we can handle. He will provide the way of escape. There is no better place to be when our backs are up against the wall than in the company of God, because He allows us to call upon Him so the world may see His faithfulness to His children. How else will they know our loving God, if they are not willing to come into His presence?

God will answer Rachel's prayers in His timing. She only needs to persevere and not give up. Our goal, like Rachel's, should be to persevere and win the race. Injuries that are not life-threatening do not keep athletes from competing. Neither should adverse circumstances stop us from receiving God's blessings when we finish our race.

In Acts 20:24, the apostle Paul said, "However, I consider my life worth nothing to me, if only I may finish the race and complete the task the Lord Jesus has given me—the task of testifying to the gospel of God's grace." Paul's desired to serve God above all else. Nothing he encountered made him stop short of accomplishing his goal.

At the end of his life, Paul could confidently say, "I have fought the good fight, I have finished the race, I have kept the faith."

Let's be encouraged as we persevere, holding on to our hope and faith in God.

# CHAPTER FOUR

---

# *Wooden Vessels: Overcoming Others with Scripture*

*See, I have engraved you on the palms of my hands; your walls are ever before me.*

Isaiah 49:16

E mily, you really know the Bible. No matter how hard I try, I just can't seem to make the time to learn Scripture like you do," said Karen.

"The Bible says we must do our best to present ourselves to God as ones approved, women who do not need to be ashamed and who correctly handle His Word. You know that's found in 2 Timothy 2:15. Further down in that chapter, it also says the Lord knows those who are His and everyone who confesses the name of the Lord must turn away from wickedness.

"Girl, we face too many temptations in our day not to learn to study God's Word. We need to know it, so we are able to call on Him and not fall into wickedness."

"I don't have time to study. When I get up, I'm running. If I'm not taking care of children, I have to concentrate on my job. Then when I get off, I'm right back where I started, focusing on my family and taking care of them. I don't have time for myself, let alone reading the Bible and learning Scripture."

"Karen, you've been my best friend for years. Don't we always make time to get together, even if it's for a little while? That's the same thing you've got to do with God. He knows your needs. You're always worried about your family and job. God says to seek first His kingdom and His righteousness, and He'll provide your needs. It's a matter of perspective."

"Emily, I'm not like you. Your faith is greater than mine. If you walked in my shoes…"

"The Bible says if you have the faith of a mustard seed, you'll be able to move mountains. You've got to give God an opportunity to show you He will take care of you."

"As I was saying, I'm doing all I can. It's easy for you to spout Scripture and tell me what a difference it would make in my life, but I don't see much difference between my life and your life. We both have problems."

"Yes, I do have problems, but I also have peace. John 14:27 comes to mind. It says, 'Peace I leave with you; my peace I give you. I do not give to you as the world gives. Do not let your hearts be troubled and do not be afraid.' That's the difference between us, Karen, God's peace. You've known me for years, and you know my problems. Have I been overcome by problems? No! If I can't control the things that come my way, why be stressed?"

"Em, I know you know Scripture and I know it gives you peace. But can't you just talk with me like you used to—before you learned so much Scripture? I need to talk with my friend without feeling as though God is against me too."

"He's not against you, Karen. It's just that I'm giving you the one lifeline that has kept me standing through the years. Without the comforting words of Scripture, I don't know whether I would still be sane. I understand the problems you face, and I understand how you feel. But I believe with all my heart that Jesus is the best thing that's ever happened to me. I'm just trying to give you the hope I've found in Him."

---

When we come into a relationship with Jesus, we decide how much time and effort we will invest in knowing and becoming like Him. We are like wooden vessels, waiting to be engraved with God's

Word. If we choose not to study and learn His Word, we are still set apart for God's use, but He is limited in how He can use us because we are empty. We can tell others about our personal experience but, because we don't know God's word, we cannot share with them its life-giving power.

Some of us may study because others view it as the right thing to do. This kind of study can be compared to fashion. Whatever is in season, is exactly what we will do. Attending Bible study groups, or developing a personal quiet time, we'll do it because that's what others say is necessary.

Some may think that quoting Scripture impresses others. It doesn't. It is not the words in Scripture that are powerful. Rather the power of Scripture comes from God, not man. He is the One who will not allow His Word to return void.

Others may study because it opens the door to a social life. They have the opportunity to be around others and make friends. Bible study is a non-threatening environment that allows them to be accepted by others in the class. They can depend on a guaranteed social outing while the study is in session.

There are some who embrace the Bible as though it were their very life. They view all of life through their understanding of Scripture. They may be self-taught, or open to any and every opinion they hear or read, making no distinction in what is written as long as the Bible is the basis for the teaching.

Some literally see the Bible as their final lifeline to life as they know it. Therefore, they desperately cling to the words of Scripture to maintain their sanity. To them, the Bible is more than a book; it is their best chance to take hold of God and His promises, to capture that abundant life which would otherwise elude them, and to live a life that pleases God.

Regardless of what we think, we should realize that our motivation to study should be to learn about God, so we are equipped to do His will. We should study to increase our personal knowledge of the Bible, or just to sharpen our memory skills.

Studying for the sole purpose of memorizing Scripture in order to win arguments, only makes us offensive and repels those to whom we are sent to give God's life-giving message. We are God's ambassadors, entrusted with His message to a dying world. Learning Scripture helps us to be faithful stewards of all He has entrusted to us.

## SCRIBES AND PHARISEES MENTALITY

Knowing and memorizing Scripture is good. If our appetite for Scripture is voracious, we need to hear, learn, and study as much as possible. However, if our sole ambition is to learn for the sake of learning, we become fat because we only ingest the Word without giving it out. If we are spiritually fat, our excess does not profit us. We must put into action what we know, so we can stay fit and trim. Taking in and giving out God's Word keeps us balanced.

The scribes were teachers of the law. *Vine's Complete Expository Dictionary of Old and New Testament Words* says the scribes "were found originally among the priests and Levites," and that "they were ambitious of honor."

Vine's also says that scribes "attached the utmost importance to ascetic elements, by which the nation was especially separated from the Gentiles," and that "In their regime, piety was reduced to external formalism." It is not a surprise that Vine's says that according to "their traditions, the Law, instead of being a help in moral and spiritual life, became an instrument for preventing true access to God,"

Luke 11:52 gives one of Jesus' comments regarding the scribes: "Woe to you experts in the law, because you have taken away the key to knowledge. You yourselves have not entered, and you have hindered those who were entering."

Again in Matthew 23:27-28, Jesus gives His opinion regarding scribes and Pharisees:

> *Woe to you, teachers of the law and Pharisees, you hypocrites! You are like whitewashed tombs, which look beautiful on the outside but on the inside are full of dead men's bones and everything unclean. In the same way, on the outside you appear to people as righteous, but on the inside you are full of hypocrisy and wickedness.*

From the above Scripture reference, we see that Jesus did not consider the Pharisees any better. "They laid stress, not upon the righteousness of an action, but upon its formal correctness," according to Vine's. A person's etiquette, formal training, or behavior, rather than his true spiritual state, determined how the religious leaders viewed him. We must be careful of looking good on the outside and being empty on the inside.

Having knowledge of Scripture, and a desire for others to know it, is commendable. Taking the time to learn Scripture shows we have a heart for God. However, we must realize that our knowledge of Scripture does not make us an authority in our lives or the lives of others. We must remember that God is in control, not us. Scripture can comfort and guide us, but it does not give us the authority to judge others or dictate what they should do in their lives.

The scribes and Pharisees were respected by the Jews, just as those of us who know and quote Scripture are sometimes held in esteem by those who don't. We may feel that our knowledge of God's Word makes us special to Him. It doesn't. Romans 2:11 says, "God does not show favoritism." Therefore we should not stumble and fall because of the status we have given ourselves based on our knowledge of Scripture.

Having God's Word engraved on our hearts provides a foundation for us to stand on when we are tested or when we are called on to give an encouraging word to others. Jesus knew and quoted Scripture when tempted by Satan in the desert. Three times, when challenged by the enemy, He spoke God's Word. Matthew 4:11 says, "Then the devil left him, and angels came and attended him."

We should know and quote Scripture also when facing temptation.

Jesus used Scripture to confront, comfort, heal, and restore. He did not hesitate to speak the truth to the scribes and Pharisees. Nor did He linger in sending words of comfort to the imprisoned John the Baptist (see Luke 7:22-23). He spoke, and the centurion's servant was healed (see Matthew 8:5-13). Who can forget His gentle restoration of Peter after His resurrection (see John 21:15-19)?

Knowledge of God's Word is power, but presenting ourselves as believers who correctly handle God's Word is even more powerful. For we are then allowing God, not our knowledge of the Word, to bring conviction and give life to others. 2 Timothy 3:16-17 says, "All Scripture is God-breathed and is useful for teaching, rebuking, correcting and training in righteousness, so that the man of God may be thoroughly equipped for every good work."

Memorizing Scripture enables us to be used by God because He is able to speak through us to others with His Word. We must remember that Satan knows Scripture, but His goal is not to use it to bring others to God. Therefore, we must not give way to the sword of the tongue but rather the sword of the Spirit so that we are used by God.

## PAUL, BEFORE THE DAMASCUS ROAD EXPERIENCE

One of the greatest persecutors of the Church, Saul, is also one of the greatest defenders of the Church, Paul. The reason he has two names is because Saul is his Jewish name, and Paul is his Greek name. Before his conversion, he was Saul the Pharisee, also the son of a Pharisee. As a Roman citizen, he automatically held a prestigious position in society. *Unger's Bible Dictionary* says, "The character of a Roman citizen superseded all others before the law and in the general opinion of society, and placed him amid the aristocracy of any provisional town."

Not only was his citizenship respected by others, but he was trained in Jerusalem by Gamaliel, one of the most distinguished teachers of the law of that day. Unger says that Saul became "more and more familiar with the outward observances of the law, and gaining that experience of the 'spirit of bondage' which should enable him to understand himself, and to teach others the blessing of the 'spirit of adoption.'" Saul knew God's Word and was confident in his understanding of the Word since he had been taught by the best.

Confidence in our knowledge does not guarantee that we are in God's will. When Stephen, a believer full of God's grace and power, was seized and taken before the Sanhedrin, everyone who looked intently at him "saw that his face was like the face of an angel" (Acts 6:15). Yet, that did not keep them from stoning him when he called them stiff-necked people with uncircumcised hearts and accused them of receiving the law but not obeying it. Saul, confident in his knowledge of the law, was there, giving approval to Stephen's death.

This led to a great persecution of the church. Saul, faithful to that which he had been taught, went from house to house, seeking to expose and destroy everyone associated with the church. Men and women were carted off to prison, and some even died. Saul's passion and zealousness in his work for God wounded, maimed, and destroyed many who truly walked with God.

We should learn from Saul. We are not God. Only God is God. We may think our knowledge of Scripture makes us more righteous than others, but that is an ungodly attitude. Our righteousness comes from God and God alone.

Although Saul was an expert in the law, it was not until he met Jesus on the Damascus road that his godly understanding of the law began. Like Saul, we can be chiseled by the greatest of teachers. But it is not until God touches us and imparts His wisdom to us that we are valuable to Him and ready to make a difference in the lives of those around us.

## PAUL AFTER THE DAMASCUS ROAD EXPERIENCE

A single encounter with Christ forever changed the proud and great persecutor of the church, Saul. He no longer saw himself as better than other believers. In fact, he placed no confidence in the flesh or any of his achievements. Christ, and Christ alone, was his desire. In Philippians 3:4-9, Paul says:

> *If anyone thinks he has reasons to put confidence in the flesh, I have more: circumcised on the eight day, of the people of Israel, of the tribe of Benjamin, a Hebrew of Hebrews; in regard to the law, a Pharisee; as for zeal, persecuting the church; as for legalistic righteousness, faultless. But whatever was to my profit I now consider loss for the sake of Christ. What is more, I consider everything a loss compared to the surpassing greatness of knowing Christ Jesus my Lord, for whose sake I have lost all things. I consider them rubbish,*

*that I may gain Christ and be found in him, not having a*
*righteousness of my own that comes from the law, but that*
*which is through faith in Christ—the righteousness that*
*comes from God and is by faith.*

We must realize that our knowledge of Scripture, our accomplishments, our birth status, or anything we take pride in outside of Christ is meaningless. Our righteousness comes from God and God alone. Before Paul met Christ on the Damascus Road, he was an expert in human knowledge. After Paul met Christ, his human knowledge was empowered and enlightened by the Holy Spirit. The wisdom of God replaced the teachings of man.

Knowledge, as defined by Webster, means, "information or understanding acquired through experience; practical ability or skill." We may think we know all the Bible says, but until we surrender to the Holy Spirit and allow Him to take what we know, give understanding to us spiritually, and massage the truths of Scripture into our hearts until we discern as God does, we have knowledge without power. God makes His Word alive in us. We are not capable of giving life to God's words.

Like Paul, we also undergo a transformation. What we think we know gives way to true instruction and understanding that is taught by God through the Holy Spirit. He refines our thinking and brings it in line with the truth of God.

Solomon had been taught by his father, David, who had also provided all the instruction and resources he needed for the construction of the temple. Yet, it was not until God gave him wisdom that he was able to carry out all that was entrusted to him.

We all have knowledge, but we must pray to God for wisdom. To become a sanctified vessel, useful to the Master, we must have His wisdom.

## WHY WE NEED GOD'S HOLY SPIRIT

Asking Jesus to come into our hearts are words anyone can say whether they mean them or not. God knows the motivations of our hearts. He knows when we are sincere and truly desire a relationship with Him. When He hears the heartfelt prayer of one who desires to come to Him, He answers their request and seals them with His Holy Spirit.

Ephesians 1:13-14 says:

*And you also were included in Christ when you heard the word of truth, the gospel of your salvation. Having believed, you were marked in him with a seal, the promised Holy Spirit, who is a deposit guaranteeing our inheritance until the redemption of those who are God's possession—to the praise of his glory.*

Some of us may wonder why Jesus isn't enough. He is. He was exactly what the disciples needed, but they didn't understand Him. Judas wanted Him to be what He wasn't. That's why he betrayed Jesus. Peter, James, and John were in His inner circle. Yet when He needed them most, they were asleep in the Garden of Gethsemane.

The twelve disciples walked with Jesus for three years, heard His teachings, and saw Him perform miracles. When Jesus died, not one remembered His teachings or His promise to send the Holy Spirit. It was not until Jesus rose from the dead and gave them the Holy Spirit, that they were prepared for the work He had given them to do.

John 20:21-22 says:

*"As the Father has sent me, I am sending you." And with that he breathed on them and said, "Receive the Holy Spirit."*

As instructed by Jesus, the apostles waited to be filled with the Holy Spirit. At Pentecost they were filled and empowered by the Holy Spirit to do the work Jesus gave them—being His witnesses in Jerusalem, and in all Judea and Samaria, and to the ends of the earth (Acts 1:8).

Scripture repeatedly tells us that Jesus was filled with the Holy Spirit. During His ministry on earth, God, the Son, never lost His connection with God, the Father, or God, the Holy Spirit. He knew His Father's heart and will and was empowered through the Holy

Spirit to accomplish God's will on earth. If we are to have Jesus' power, we must also be filled with the Holy Spirit to accomplish the work God has given us.

Our own understanding or interpretation of the Bible is not to be relied upon. The disciples were taught by God, the Son, and yet they failed to understand His words. Why should we consider ourselves better than them? Until we are filled with the Holy Spirit, our words have no power.

And how do we get the Holy Spirit? Jesus answers that question for us in Luke 11:13: "If you then, though you are evil, know how to give good gifts to your children, how much more will your Father in heaven give the Holy Spirit to those who ask him!"

Even though we have the Holy Spirit, we may not always feel that we are adequately prepared to handle any situation God allows in our lives. If God's Word is engraved on our hearts, we need to trust Him to correctly use his Words. Jesus encourages us in Luke 12:11-12 when He says, "Do not worry about how you will defend yourselves or what you will say, for the Holy Spirit will teach you at that time what you should say."

Be encouraged. Know that we are not in control. God is!

Sealing us for the day of redemption and empowering us are not the only things the Holy Spirit does for us. We can feast on the gifts He gives us in Galatians 5:22-23: "Love, joy, peace, patience, kindness, goodness, faithfulness, gentleness and self-control."

In the Old Testament, the Holy Spirit indwelled people temporarily. That is not the case in the New Testament. The Holy Spirit freely gives us insight and understanding of Scripture, comforts us, brings Scripture to mind, empowers us to do God's work, gives us discernment, testifies to our spirits, and intercedes for us with groans when we do not know what to pray. All this is available to us as long as we submit to God and are daily filled with His Spirit.

## PERSONAL APPLICATION

At the beginning of this chapter, Emily's desire was to comfort her best friend with Scripture. God's Word had given her comfort during difficult times, and she wanted her friend to share that experience. The difference between our words of comfort and God's Word is that His Word is powerful. God ministered to Emily through His Holy Spirit as she read and studied His Word.

Emily went to God and received the healing she needed during stressful times in her life. She knew God had heard and answered her prayer, and she wanted her best friend to know God's goodness. However, during our initial walk with God, He is building our trust in Him. When Jesus sent out the seventy-two disciples in Luke 10, He was laying the foundation for their faith. He allowed them to participate in and witness His miracles, so they could learn to trust Him.

As wooden vessels being engraved by God, we have His attention focused on us. He's strengthening our tie to Him through answered prayers, restoration, and knowledge of Him. He develops our love for Him as we commune with Him. He wants to draw us close so we can know Him as Jesus knew Him. This is our personal time with God.

We may know the value of Scripture, but we may not know how to express the comfort we receive from reading the Bible to others. We tell ourselves that they would understand how we feel if they only read the Word. For Scripture to quicken the hearts of those who read it, they must be in a right relationship with God. There is often nothing we can do or say that will give life to God's Word in the hearts of others.

When we begin our walk with God and are filled with the Holy Spirit, we may discover that as we study Scripture God gives us only enough for ourselves. Newborn babies do not give their bottles to others. They need all the nourishment that is offered them. They feed at their mother's breast or hand until satisfied.

God knows we don't know Him or His Word. Therefore, as we study to learn of Him, He opens Scripture and reveals Himself to us until we are satisfied. Like newborn babies, our intake initially is limited but increases as we grow in the knowledge of Him.

We may try to share with others before we are full of God, and we wonder why we have little effect on them. We can't give what we don't have. Until we have grown in our relationship with and understanding of God, we can only tell others how we feel. Our passion for God is still growing and may not be full enough to spill over into the lives of others. We share out of our excess. Scripture says Jesus was filled with the Holy Spirit and that the disciples were filled with the Holy Spirit. If we don't know God, and we learn about Him through His Word, what do we have to share with others that will change their lives?

We should not be surprised or feel rejected if others don't respond in the way we desire when we share God's Word. Paul wrote to the Corinthians: "My message and my preaching were not with wise and persuasive words, but with a demonstration of the Spirit's power, so that your faith might not rest on men's wisdom, but on God's power." It is not our job to convince or persuade others to accept God's Word. God knows those who are His and will draw them to Him in His timing.

We cannot spiritually know all those who belong to God. Therefore, when God prompts us to speak His Word, we must be obedient. Paul did not hesitate to tell King Agrippa about Jesus. King Agrippa's response to Paul's passionate testimony is recorded in Acts 26:28:

*"Do you think that in such a short time you can persuade me to be a Christian?"*

We must trust that God's Word will always bear fruit in the hearts of believers.

Isaiah 55:6-11 says:

*Seek the Lord while he may be found; call on him while he is near. Let the wicked forsake his way and the evil man his thoughts. Let him turn to the Lord, and he will have mercy on him, and to our God, for he will freely pardon. As the heavens are higher than the earth, so are my ways higher than your ways and my thoughts than your thoughts. As the rain and the snow come down from heaven, and do not return to it without watering the earth and making it bud*

*and flourish, so that it yields seed for the sower and bread*
*for the eater, so is my word that goes out from my mouth: It*
*will not return to me empty, but will accomplish what I*
*desire and achieve the purpose for which I sent it.*

Karen could not see Emily's peace, but she could see the problems Emily faced and her responses to those problems. When people are hurting, they may not be seeking someone to preach to them. But they are more likely to respond to a peaceful spirit and gentle words.

People may feel they can relate to us when we share common experiences. However, they will not be able to relate to us spiritually if they do not know Christ. Sharing His Word gives others an opportunity to hear of Him, but it does not guarantee that they will turn from their wicked ways and come to Him. Our desire to see others saved does not guarantee their salvation.

Like Emily, we can share Scripture with others, but we cannot dictate their response. We can give our testimony to illustrate the Scripture we share. Only when others see a genuine change in us will some seek to know the cause.

People were leery of Paul after his conversion experience, because they knew what he had done before he met Jesus. His previous comrades did not trust him because he no longer carried out his zealous persecution of the Church. Believers did not trust him because of his previous harsh treatment of them.

Fear of Paul must have been great, especially if Ananias chose to take the time to make God aware of who it was He sent him to minister to. When we think God has made a mistake or does not have our best interest at heart, we take the time to discuss the situation with Him also. Our discussion can be the same as Ananias' in Acts 9:10-16

*"Ananias!"*
*"Yes, Lord."*
*"Go to the house of Judas on Straight Street and ask for a*
*man from Tarsus named Saul, who is praying."*

*"Lord, I have heard many reports about this man and all the harm he has done to your saints in Jerusalem. And he has come here with authority from the chief priests to arrest all who call on your name."*
*But the Lord said to Ananias, "Go! This man is my chosen instrument to carry my name before the Gentiles and their kings and before the people of Israel. I will show him how much he must suffer for my name."*

Arguing with God accomplishes nothing. It only delays our obedience. Delayed obedience is disobedience because we are not fulfilling God's will for our lives. When God calls us to share His Word with others, we must do it, regardless of our opinion of them. He knows who will cross our paths and when they will do it. He only needs for us to be ready to share His Word as it says it 2 Timothy 4:2: "Preach the Word; be prepared in season and out of season; correct, rebuke and encourage—with great patience and careful instruction."

# CHAPTER FIVE

## *Problems: Who Needs Them?*

### Submission

W hy do you always challenge everything I say? Don't you trust me to make the right decisions for our family?" asked Fred as he stared at his wife, Sandra, across the dining room table.

With her arms firmly pressed against her chest, Sandra shifted her body to rest against the back of her chair. She turned her head slightly to break eye contact momentarily, then returned Fred's stare. "Yes, I do trust you to make right decisions for our family when you have our family's best interest at heart. But the majority of the time you make decisions based on what you want, Fred. Then you expect everyone to go along with your plans, whether we like them or not. That's not fair or right!"

"Fair or right? What's fair or right about me catching flak from you every time you don't agree with my decisions? You can't have it both ways. Either you're with me or you're not. Sandra, I need to know you're in my corner and will support me in all I do."

"What about me, Fred? Shouldn't my concerns be considered before you make decisions for our family? I made good decisions before we were married, so why can't you value my opinions now?

Marriage didn't take away my ability to think. My opinions may sometimes differ from yours, but that doesn't mean they're wrong."

"Sandra, I'm not saying your opinions aren't valid, but only one of us can make decisions for our family. Since I'm the man, that responsibility belongs to me. I'm the one who will be held accountable before God, so why can't you go along with the decisions I make?"

"I can't believe you would say those words. You aren't the only one affected by the decisions you make. We all are. Therefore, why shouldn't you consider my input? God may have given you the final say-so in the decision-making process, but He certainly didn't intend for you to exclude my opinions. If man could do everything by himself, why would God have wasted His time creating woman?" Glaring at Fred, Sandra pushed her chair back, arose, and hastily left the room.

Fred sat quietly in his chair and flinched when he heard the bedroom door slam. "She doesn't understand my role," he mumbled.

---

Many of us can identify with either Fred or Sandra, whether we're married or not, because we've probably heard someone's personal story that is similar to theirs. Yet, our problem with submission does not begin in our earthly relationships, but rather in our relationship with God.

To become a vessel of honor, sanctified, and useful to the Master, we must choose to submit to Him. Until we submit to Him, we are in rebellion, even if we have asked Jesus to be Lord and Savior of our lives.

## SUBMISSION DEFINED

Submission is not a difficult word to say. However, submission is challenging to practice, especially on a daily basis. According to Webster, submission is "a yielding to the power or authority of another; obedience; the spirit of subjection or obedience; an acquiescent temper; humility; resignation; meekness." If someone desired to form a line of those who desired submission, it is hard to envision anything other than an extremely short line.

Have you ever wondered why Jesus did not have a problem submitting to His Father? It is because He knew God, understood God's purpose for Him, and he agreed with God's purpose for His life. Knowing God and agreeing with Him gives us freedom to submit, yield, or obey because we know that God, not people, is in control. Therefore, we are not threatened by the decisions of others, because our trust is in God's sovereignty, not in the actions of others.

Before complete submission takes place in our lives, we must know and trust the sovereignty of God. It is almost impossible not to be concerned for ourselves if we are unsure of God's ability to protect us in all situations. The man Job seems foolish to a person who cannot understand why he would continue to trust a God who allowed everything he had to be taken away. But Job's trust in God reveals his core beliefs. When all that we rely upon is stripped away, with nothing to take its place, our beliefs will determine our response in situations.

Abraham's willingness to sacrifice his only son, when he knew his wife could not produce another child, appears ludicrous to one who desires to be in control. Choosing to submit to the will of another, when it conflicts with personal passions and desires, may cause severe emotional stress. We cannot support what we do not truly believe when our lives or the lives of our loved ones are at stake.

Israel's first king, Saul, was chosen by the people. Because of disobedience, God rejected him and told the prophet Samuel to anoint David to replace him. Time after time, Saul attempted to kill David, yet was unsuccessful.

David had several opportunities to kill King Saul, but he refused to do so. Why would he refuse to kill the man who wrongfully sought to end his life? He refused to lay a hand against God's anointed.

Saul may have been anointed but David's son, Absalom, was not. He stole the hearts of the Israelites, overthrew his father's kingdom, and had plans to kill his father. Yet David felt compassion for his son and did not desire his death.

Are we willing to trust that God is in control even when we're under attack from close friends and family? Do we have a heart of compassion for those He may be using as refining fire in our lives?

What did these men know about God that caused them to submit to trials that must have challenged their core beliefs in Him? Surely their emotions and thoughts wreaked havoc on their physical bodies. They aren't any different from us. Yet, their choices during stressful times force us to look at ourselves and see if we are as devoted to God and willing to submit to Him, regardless of our trying circumstances.

Knowing God and trusting in His goodness are different from knowing of God and hearing of His goodness to others. J. I. Packer in *Knowing God* says:

> *Knowing God involves, first, listening to God's Word and receiving it as the Holy Spirit interprets it, in application to oneself; second, noting God's nature and character, as his Word and works reveal it; third, accepting his invitations and doing what he commands; fourth, recognizing and rejoicing in the love that he has shown in thus approaching you and drawing you into this divine fellowship.*

This is more than a mental assent to belief in God. Packer's statement suggests that a person's mind, will, emotions, and body are involved in becoming intimately acquainted with God. The focus is not upon carrying out our own will or desires but rather knowing God and doing what pleases Him. Our belief in the Creator of the universe and obedience to Him must be greater than our belief in what we see. Job, Abraham, and David rested firmly in their faith in God, despite the circumstances in their lives.

Packer also says:

> *The knower 'looks up' to the one known, and the latter takes responsibility for the welfare of the former. This is part of the biblical concept of knowing God, that those who know him—that is, those by whom he allows himself to be known—are loved and cared for by him.*

Everyone who knows God must assume that He loves and cares for us. The difficulty arises when we experience trying circumstances in our lives, especially when we think we are being obedient to God's Word or man's laws. We must not waver in faith, but remain steadfast, and cling to the words of Jeremiah 29:11: "'For I know the plans I have for you,' says the Lord, 'Plans for good and not for evil, to give you a future and a hope.'" Until we are ready to seek God's will at all costs, we will struggle with selfish interests and desires.

## THE "ME" FACTOR

Many enter into a relationship with expectations of strengthening and nurturing ties already formed. Initially, an effort is made to accommodate the desires of another. Over the passage of time, the truth of the old adage, "familiarity breeds contempt," can seep into the relationship. What was once cute or funny about a person becomes intolerable or stupid, especially during times of conflict.

The silent killer of relationships is the "Me" factor. A person usually enters a relationship in the "us" mode—seeking to meet the needs of the other person, doing what the other person likes, and putting the other person first. After the "connection" has been sealed and both parties are satisfied with the other, old habits slip in, and people often begin to seek and satisfy their own selfish interests. Focus is no longer on meeting the needs or desires of the other person, but rather on meeting one's own needs and desires.

Selfish motives can destroy rather than build up a relationship. It is hard for us to humble ourselves and put another person first if we believe our needs are most important. Therefore true submission in relationships is seldom achieved without submission to Christ first.

Unfortunately, it appears that some people carry this same mindset into their relationship with God. Initially we desire to know God and do what pleases Him. As time passes, we often revert to old ways—putting self, not God, first. This is not submission to God. Barging ahead and fulfilling personal desires without consulting or heeding God's Word is not the way to build and sustain a positive relationship with God. Self-exaltation destroys a submissive spirit, whether in human or godly relationships. It can be likened to Simon, who thought he could buy the gift of the Holy Spirit for his own glory in Acts 8:18-24.

## GODLY SUBMISSION

Submission requires that we know God's purpose for our lives. God reveals Himself through the Bible. Only when we personally read and study God's Word can we know God's boundaries and how to respond to life's situations. God allows His Holy Spirit to give life to His Word as it is studied so we can have the wisdom and insight to correctly apply Scripture to our lives. As long as we choose to put God first, God is faithful to His Word. Proverbs 3:5-6 says, "Trust in the Lord with all your heart and lean not on your own understanding; in all your ways acknowledge him, and he will make your paths straight." We cannot exalt ourselves and exalt God at the same time. A decision must be made as to who will be in control of our lives—God or self.

If God is to be in control of our lives, then He must be in control of every aspect of our lives: marriage, work, friendships, home, and even vacations. We must choose to put God first in every area of our lives. Once that decision is made, the door is open for us to respond as Job, Abraham, and David did.

Submission without obedience is meaningless, as Samuel told Saul in 1 Samuel 15:22: "Does the Lord delight in burnt offerings and sacrifices as much as in obeying the voice of the Lord? To obey is better than sacrifice, and to heed is better than the fat of rams." We, like the Israelites, can outwardly obey God, but still remain rebellious inwardly. God desires submission of our will, which leads to a change in our actions.

Although Jesus is God, while on earth He humbled Himself and obeyed His Father's purpose for His life. Philippians 2:5-11 states:

*Your attitude should be the same as that of Christ Jesus:*
*Who, being in very nature God, did not consider equality*

*with God something to be grasped, but made himself noth-*
*ing, taking the very nature of a servant, being made in*
*human likeness. And being found in appearance as a man,*
*he humbled himself and became obedient to death—even*
*death on a cross! Therefore God exalted him to the highest*
*place and gave him the name that is above every name, that*
*at the name of Jesus every knee should bow, in heaven, and*
*on earth, and every tongue confess that Jesus Christ is Lord,*
*to the glory of God the Father.*

He obeyed His Father because He is one with the Father. If we are one with God, we must also choose to submit to Him in obedience.

Even though Job did not understand God's purpose in allowing the destruction of his children and all he owned, he did not sway from his faith in God. Could that have been why God allowed Satan to test him, because He knew Job would remain faithful? Would we be able to pass such a test if God allowed us to be tested in the same manner?

Abraham loved his son more than all his wealth; yet he responded in obedience to God's Word. Abraham's love for God superseded his love for Isaac. Jesus requires the same from His disciples. In Luke 14:26, He says, "If anyone comes to me and does not hate his father and mother, his wife and children, his brothers and sisters—yes, even his own life—he cannot be my disciple." If God is the same yesterday, today, and tomorrow, why should we be surprised that He requires us to make the same decision?

David was anointed by Samuel and knew he would be king; yet he refused to be the one to depose Saul, God's first-chosen king. Since David's security was in God, not man, he trusted God to do exactly as He promised. David was content to wait for God's timing, trusting God to protect him in the meantime, and depose Saul. Waiting for God to do what He says sometimes challenges our patience and our trust in Him.

A new believer may struggle at this point because he or she is not yet experienced in putting God first in all things. That's why a new believer is like a clay vessel—raw and unrefined. However, as he matures in his walk with God, he learns obedience and begins to put God first.

Maturing believers should realize that submission is not a one time event. Daily, we need to put God first. Even the apostle Paul experienced this struggle. In Romans 7:7-25 he explains the struggle between his inner being and his physical body.

Bringing the body, will, and mind into agreement with God's purpose for our lives can be difficult but rewarding when we achieve discipline. Our relationship with God determines our response to submission. If the Holy Spirit indwells us, our lives should be changed. However, that does not mean we will not sin. We will, but we will not have a continual lifestyle of sin.

## Why God Chastens

Observing people's actions allows us to see if their actions match their words. Few people are deceived when a person claims to do one thing, yet does another. A child cannot lie successfully to parents when the parents know his or her actions. A student who lies about studying will be exposed by a pop quiz. A spouse cannot conceal secret purchases when the bank or credit card statement arrives. An employee cannot claim quality production when work is sloppily done or incompetent. Neither can we claim to walk with God if we remain fruitless.

Webster defines chasten as "to discipline by punishment or affliction; chastise to moderate; soften; temper; to refine; purify." *Vine's Complete Expository Dictionary of Old and New Testament Words* defines chasten as, "To train children; to chastise whether (a) by correcting with words, reproving, and admonishing, or (b) by 'chastening' by the infliction of evils and calamities."

Children who have been trained to obey while young are usually less likely to act out and do as they please when older, because the limits for proper behavior were established in their youth. The child knows what is and is not acceptable. The same is true with a new hire in the workforce. There is usually a probation period to see if the employee and the employer are a "good fit." During this trial period, the employee may receive "warnings" if his or her behavior is inappropriate. This gives the employee the opportunity to adhere to what the employer wants or to seek employment elsewhere if unwilling to change.

Relationships are no different. Each person decides what he or she can tolerate, and informs the other person of that decision. When one person continually ignores or blatantly violates the acceptable limitations of the other, the relationship is in jeopardy and may not last long. If guidelines are necessary in human relationships to ensure harmony and a nurturing environment, why would God accept less, especially if believers are to be His ambassadors on earth?

Paul's instructions to Titus are given in Titus 2:11-14:

> *For the grace of God that brings salvation has appeared to all men. It teaches us to say "No" to ungodliness and worldly passions, and to live self-controlled, upright and godly lives in this present age, while we wait for the blessed hope—the glorious appearing of our great God and Savior, Jesus Christ, who gave himself for us to redeem us from all wickedness and to purify for himself a people that are his very own, eager to do what is good.*

Discipline teaches believers to say "No" to things that entice us to sin so our talk about Jesus and our walk with Him can be the same. Just as an earthly parent seeks to break a child's bad habit, so does God. He allows circumstances in our lives to make us aware of sin in our lives. We can then either agree with God about the sin in our lives and choose to obey Him, or continue sinning. We cannot choose to willfully sin without suffering the consequences. Not only are there human consequences, but there are also spiritual consequences, because the Holy Spirit is quenched when we sin.

God chose King David to lead Israel. Yet David says in Psalm 32:3-5:

> *When I kept silent, my bones wasted away through my groaning all day long. For day and night your hand was heavy upon me; my strength was sapped as in the heat of*

*summer. Then I acknowledged my sin to you and did not*
*cover up my iniquity. I said, 'I will confess my transgressions*
*to the Lord'—and you forgave the guilt of my sin.*

Physically and spiritually David suffered when he chose not to submit to God's will. If David suffered despite being chosen by God, why should we as believers feel we will escape God's discipline? Hebrews 12:6 says that God disciplines those He loves and punishes those who are His. How else will He weed out behavior that is not of Him?

God can use anyone to accomplish His purposes on earth. However, people He can use as examples for others to follow must have hearts that yield and submit to Him. Yielded and submitted believers are examples of silver and gold vessels. God does not leave us in our clay state. Chastening transforms us from clay to wooden vessels. God's refining process turns us from wood to silver to gold, as we are conformed into the image of His Son, Jesus Christ. James 1:22-25 says:

*Do not merely listen to the word, and so deceive yourselves.*
*Do what it says. Anyone who listens to the word but does*
*not do what it says is like a man who looks at his face in a*
*mirror and, after looking at himself, goes away and imme-*
*diately forgets what he looks like. But the man who looks*
*intently into the perfect law that gives freedom, and contin-*
*ues to do this, not forgetting what he has heard, but doing*
*it—he will be blessed in what he does.*

## COMMITMENT DETERMINES SUBMISSION

An individual can know the value of exercise and a healthy diet, but that does not guarantee he will practice what he knows. Or a person may know the value of encouraging words and yet choose not to speak them. These people are no different from the person who knows God's Word but does not obey. The core problem is a lack of commitment to what is known and/or a lack of desire to submit to that knowledge.

The newest restaurant, department store, or movie attracts many. So does the latest fad diet or exercise program. However, interest fades once the newness leaves if a lifestyle change has not occurred. A person not committed to juicing, will only juice for a short period of time. Those who like meat will certainly not last long on a vegetarian diet. Seldom will a couch potato become physically fit. Why would a person who does not practice God's Word fully submit to Him? God's Word should produce a lifestyle, not temporary changes, in an individual's life.

Entering a new relationship and maintaining the same negative behavior as before shortchanges the other person involved. A woman does not want her spouse or significant other to act as though she doesn't exist. Nor does a man want his spouse or significant other to consider him or his opinions as worthless. That is not the basis for a loving relationship. According to 1 Corinthians 13:4-8:

> *Love is patient, love is kind. It does not envy, it does not boast, it is not proud. It is not rude, it is not self-seeking, it is not easily angered, it keeps no record of wrongs. Love does not delight in evil but rejoices with the truth. It always protects, always trusts, always hopes, always perseveres. Love never fails.*

Love is the door that allows one to submit to God and then to others.

Without love for God, an individual cannot put Him first or trust Him to make all things work together for good. Instead the person will seek to tell God how to respond in a situation or how to answer a prayer if that person does not submit to Him. It's not that the individual sees himself as better than God, but that he still believes he knows what is best in any given situation. This is evident when an individual does not consult God first, but charges ahead, only to discover that his solution does not fix the problem.

Most people have the same problem as the toddler who thinks the world revolves around him or her. It is not until an individual submits to the wisdom of God, as a toddler submits to the wisdom of the parent, that positive growth can occur. God, like a good parent, has the best interest of His child at heart and will not allow His child to be overcome by circumstances.

He knows what to allow in our lives to conform us to His image. And like a good parent, He allows us to learn from difficult circumstances in life, instead of providing a problem-free life for us. As with the toddler, juvenile, or teen, submission is necessary if we are to enjoy the fruit of God.

God's good fruit is listed in Galatians 5:22-23: "love, joy, peace, patience, kindness, goodness, faithfulness, gentleness and self-control." However the bad fruit of wickedness is also listed in Galatians 5:19-21: "sexual immorality, impurity and debauchery, idolatry and witchcraft, hatred, discord, jealousy, fits of rage, selfish ambition, dissensions, factions and envy; drunkenness, orgies, and the like."

Our fruit demonstrates whether or not we are submitted to God. Selfish motives or desires reign in our hearts when we are not submitted to God. When we make God's kingdom and His righteousness a priority in our lives, then we love God enough to submit to His will.

## SUBMISSION UNTO DEATH

True submission begins with God. We cannot submit to anyone or anything if we are not in submission to Him. Job had to submit to God in order to say, "Though he slay me, yet will I hope in him," (Job 13:15) because it is not our nature to endure such personal hardship without looking for the cause and stopping it. When we really put God first, we'll entrust Him with our hearts because we know He will take care of us.

Our confidence in God's care for us should stem from Isaiah 49:15-16: "Can a mother forget the baby at her breast and have no compassion on the child she has borne? Though she may forget, I will not forget you! See, I have engraved you on the palms of my hands; your walls are ever before me." If we believe God is all-powerful, has knowledge of everything, and is in control of all things, why should we hesitate to trust Him with our lives and bow the knee in complete submission to His will for our lives?

When we love someone, it is not hard for us to imagine ourselves with that person, or for us to look out for the welfare of our loved one. That's one of the reasons a young girl writes the name of her loved one on the palm of her hand, or on anything else that is convenient. If God has engraved us on the palm of His hand, then we should know He loves us.

However, we must realize the difference between our submission to all God allows in our lives and submission to what we think is best for our lives. Submission to our mates honors God. Yet, if we intentionally marry or align ourselves with those who choose not to put God first, we may suffer great struggles.

A mother of eleven children chose to leave her husband. For years, she had submitted to his will. Because she did not share her reasons for leaving her husband with her children, one of them turned on the light in the room where the mother hid when the father made an unexpected visit one night. As the mother tried to leave the room, the father shot her in the back as his children watched.

Leaving did not guarantee the safety of the mother, nor did it bring healing to the family. The father was executed a year later. We must be extremely careful when entrusting our hearts to others. God gave us life; therefore, we should value and preserve it.

2 Corinthians 6:14-16 says:

*Do not be yoked together with unbelievers. For what do righteousness and wickedness have in common? Or what fellowship can light have with darkness? What harmony is there between Christ and Belial? What does a believer have in common with an unbeliever? What agreement is there between the temple of God and idols? For we are the temple of the living God. As God has said: "I will live with them and walk among them, and I will be their God, and they will be my people."*

Giving our hearts to those who do not know God opens us to things we may not want to experience, such as the acts of the sinful nature listed in Galatians 5:19-21: "Sexual immorality, impurity and debauchery; idolatry and witchcraft; hatred, discord, jealousy, fits of rage, selfish ambition, dissensions, factions and envy; drunkenness, orgies, and the like."

By no means is this list reserved exclusively for non-Christians because there are those who call themselves Christians who are guilty of these acts. Then there are those who are nonbelievers whose actions are godlier than believers. Our best means of discernment is to seek God's face in prayer regarding the person on earth to whose hand we entrust our hearts. If we fear the person will not protect and guard our hearts as God promises He will do in His Word, then we should be very careful in making such alliances.

Some seek refuge in shelters to escape abusive situations because the ones to whom they entrusted their hearts have not loved them with the love of Christ, a self-sacrificial, other-centered love. Instead, their mates may use them as objects on which to vent their frustration, anger, or anxiety. Nowhere in Scripture does God require us to submit unto death. He asked Abraham to take his son, his only son, to a mountain in the region of Moriah and kill him. Yet, as Abraham raised his hand in obedience to slay his son, God stopped him. God provided a way of escape, a ram in the bush, to be sacrificed instead of Abraham's son.

Submission to God and obedience to His Word should be our goals. Suffering the consequences of our actions, like Jonah who was in the belly of a fish three days and three nights, cannot be blamed on God. Spouses in abusive situations may have brain damage from physical abuse, chemical changes in their brain from depression, or lack role models for healthy behavior. Unless they are willing to completely expose their situation to counselors trained in handling abusive relationships, their submission may lead to death. We must not mistake submission to sinful people as God's best for our lives. If we willingly choose to put ourselves in such situations, we should not blame God when suffering the consequences of our actions.

God loves us and desires our best, but He also gives us freedom to choose the path we desire to travel. That's why the author stresses that we must submit to God in all situations. As He protected and provided for David when his son, Absalom, tried to wrench the kingdom from his hands, God will take care of us if we are in His will.

## PERSONAL APPLICATION

At the beginning of this chapter, Fred and Sandra struggled with submission in their marriage. Fred felt Sandra should honor his role as head of the home and support the decisions he made. Sandra felt that Fred should seek her input and value it before making a final decision. She thought Fred's decisions reflected his selfish interests, rather than what was best for the family. Their conversation ended with broken communication and both parties dissatisfied.

Problems arise in relationships when people choose not to put God first or do things His way. Even though Sandra may have been right in her comments to Fred, her actions did not bring about a godly resolution to the problem. Nor was her family blessed by her actions. Sandra must learn to submit to those God has placed in authority over her. That includes her husband, her boss, police officers, government officials, and even her pastor.

What if a person is abusive? Scripture does not tell of an abusive God who seeks to destroy those He created. Those bound by sin may abuse, but God doesn't. He never allows His children to suffer more than they can bear. That's why He always provides a way of escape. When God opens a door of escape, we are to take it.

Selfishness is not the same as abuse. Sandra's life was not threatened by Fred's decisions. Therefore, she could go to God in prayer and wait for Him to intercede. The same opportunity to pray and wait for God was available to Fred. We always have access to God through prayer. We can talk with Him about any person or situation. In His timing, He will bring about a solution that is best for all involved.

In 1 Samuel 25, Abigail had a fool for a husband. Everyone in his household knew his disposition. Yet, when the lives of the males in her household were threatened, Abigail quickly acted in a manner that saved their lives without the knowledge of her husband. She received the favor of all in her household, as well as King David and his men.

If Sandra doubted that Fred's heart was in the hand of God, she should pray to God and allow Him to work in her circumstances according to His will and His timing. God does not change. As He brought about a favorable solution to Abigail's problem, He will certainly hear and answer Sandra's prayer requests in a way that honors Him. God can strengthen Sandra's belief in Him if she asks. She must first acknowledge her unbelief as the man did in Mark 9:24. God, not Fred, is in control.

There is the possibility that some wives may not want to submit to their husbands or anyone else. 1 Peter 2:13-17 says:

*Submit yourselves for the Lord's sake to every authority instituted among men: whether to the king, as the supreme authority, or to governors, who are sent by him to punish those who do wrong and to commend those who do right. For it is God's will that by doing good you should silence the ignorant talk of foolish men. Live as free men, but do not use your freedom as a coverup for evil; live as servants of God. Show proper respect to everyone.*

Vengeance belongs to God, not man, as Romans 12:17-19 says. When we are filled with the Holy Spirit, we can cast our cares upon Jesus and trust that He has everything under control. Therefore, true submission to human authority is done for God's sake, and shows our obedience to His Word, despite circumstances or difficulties.

Fred used his God-given role as head of the house to fulfill his selfish desires. When God places us in positions of authority, it is not for us to lord that position over others, as 1 Peter 5:3 says. A great leader serves those entrusted to his care. Those of us who use a position of leadership to only meet our needs, do not find favor with others or God. Leaders must realize they are only God's servants. Leaders must also realize they are held to a higher standard of judgment. Therefore, the role of leadership should not be taken lightly.

In Ephesians 5:25, God commands husbands to love their wives as Christ loved the church. Jesus did not browbeat the church into submission to Him, neither did He control through manipulation. Rather He gave up His life to bring the church into a right relationship with God. He showed His love through His actions as well as His words. He did not hesitate to stoop and wash the disciples' feet, even though He was the guest of honor. He laid aside the honor and respect He should have received on earth so others could see, know, and love His Father.

When Fred grows to the point of laying aside his needs and loving Sandra as much as he loves himself, God will be honored in their relationship.

In Job 2:9, when Job's wife said: "Are you still holding onto your integrity? Curse God and die!" it does not seem that she was spiritually sensitive to his needs. Yet Job did not allow her discouraging words to dissuade him from submitting to the hard times God allowed in his life. His obedience brought about the restoration of his earthly goods, favor with others, and God's blessing of more children. Since God is the same yesterday, today, and tomorrow, He will continue to sustain and bless those who are submitted and obedient to Him, regardless of life's situations.

Fred and Sandra's obedience and submission to God will resolve the differences in their relationship. Neither can expect God's blessing in their lives if they are not submitted to Him.

# CHAPTER SIX

# Silver Vessels: Beginning to Shine

*And the words of the Lord are flawless, like silver refined in a furnace of clay, purified seven times.*

Psalm 12:6

I'm so tired of hearing people say, 'That's how I am. You can either accept me as I am or not. I'm not changing.' What makes them think they are so valuable as is?" asked Jackie.

"Yeah," replied Rhonda, "Don't they know when you buy something 'as is,' it usually means it's broken and needs repair?"

"I've been working in this job training program for twenty years. Whenever we receive students who think their way is best and that they are not in need of change, we know there is nothing we can do for them. Do you have those same problems in counseling?" asked Jackie.

"As long as there are people, we will have those problems. It doesn't matter what field you're in. People are people, and until they recognize the need for change, they think they are acceptable as is. Can you imagine us telling God that? 'God, if you want me to serve you, You have to take me "as is," and I want the best position you have,'" said Rhonda as she laughed.

"You say that as a joke, but that's the way many people approach their relationship with God. They think that once they have accepted Jesus in their hearts, that's all they need to do. They feel God should be honored they have turned to Him, and they wait for Him to exalt them to positions of honor, even if they don't know anything about Him."

"That reminds me of the television program I saw showing how silver is refined. Did you know that silver is bathed?"

"Makes sense to me. Who wants to deal with unnecessary dirt?"

"Not me!" said Rhonda, "I've got my hands full keeping myself clean," she said as she smiled. "In its natural state, silver is impure and bound up with other substances. It has worth but not much value. Can you imagine how attractive a clump of ore would be, or wearing a ring made of silver dust?"

"That's not exactly the kind of jewelry I'd buy," said Jackie.

"Only when silver has been through the furnace, at extremely high temperatures, is it ready to be separated from what accompanies it."

"What happens next?" inquired Jackie.

"When it comes out of the furnace, it is tested to determine the silver content. If there is not enough silver, it has to go through the process again."

"I wouldn't want to endure that heat again. I'd try to have as much silver in me as possible," said Jackie.

"The silver content depends on the source—lead, copper, zinc or scraps."

"All this is so complicated! What made you watch the television show?" asked Jackie.

"I don't know, but once I started watching, it reminded me of our relationship with God. Let me finish explaining the process because I want to tell you how it ends. After enduring that whole process, silver has another step to go through. It must be polished so that it has the right reflection for its intended purpose."

"Who would have thought it takes so much work to produce the silver I take for granted!" said Jackie.

––––––––––

It is not surprising that Rhonda equated the refining process of silver to God's work on us. In fact, Malachi 3:2-3 says:

*But who can endure the day of his coming? Who can stand when he appears? For he will be like a refiner's fire or a launderer's soap. He will sit as a refiner and purifier of silver; he will purify the Levites and refine them like gold and silver. Then the Lord will have men who will bring offerings in righteousness.*

Refining fire and a launderer's soap both refer to the cleansing process. God sees our value, but before He can use us greatly, we must first be purified.

The refining process tests our submission to God. When difficulties arise, our true beliefs are revealed. As the saying goes: "We behave as we behave because we believe as we believe." We may be surprised by our behavior, but God is not.

In Malachi's time, the Levites were God's priests, but today it is those of us who have accepted Jesus as Savior who are God's priests. In 1 Peter 2:5, Scripture tells us, "You also, like living stones, are being built into a spiritual house to be a holy priesthood, offering spiritual sacrifices acceptable to God through Jesus Christ." Peter then says: "You are a chosen people, a royal priesthood, a holy nation, a people belonging to God, that you may declare the praises of him who called you out of darkness into his wonderful light" (1 Peter 2:9). We should expect God to cleanse, refine, and mold us according to His purpose for our lives, as He did with His priests in Malachi's time.

## WHAT HAPPENED TO THE GOOD LIFE?

When we first enter our relationship with Jesus, some of us may assume the difficulties we once experienced are over. We may look to Him to protect us from bad things that may come our way. However, that way of thinking is not Biblical. Rather, it may reflect our belief in the "happily ever after" fairy tales.

We may harbor the idea that Jesus is our friend. We all know that friends, especially best friends, are always there to see us through. We can count on their loyalty and commitment. Therefore, with Jesus as our best friend, problems will not overcome us. In fact, sometimes we think our difficult days are over, and that we are on the road to a problem-free life. Fantasy! Pure fantasy!

When we are saved, God is gracious to us. He doesn't bombard us with spiritual problems because we haven't learned to trust Him. However, that does not mean we are insulated from what others may do to us. The difference is that we are no longer stressed because of our circumstances or situations.

As we study God's Word and begin to know Him, He may allow little difficulties in our lives just to let us know He is faithful to His Word. Once we trust Him and know that He is faithful, we are ready for His refining process.

God washed us with the blood of Jesus when we came to Him. He then started His refining process in us, in effect, turning up the heat on us, by allowing little problems that made us aware of sin areas in our lives. Hopefully, we went to His Word and received comfort and guidance. To our surprise, we discovered that God is all He claims to be. What a relief!

Initial success in the refining process may cause us to feel that we can withstand anything God allows in our lives. A confident and successful elementary student is not necessarily ready for what will be encountered as a teen or an adult. It is only when we are in a situation that we know what our response is and if we have passed the test. Any other attitude can be seen as pride—the stumbling block before our fall.

We may view problems, especially those caused by others, as something to be avoided. Seldom do we see them as opportunities to grow spiritually. However, if we believe that God is really in control, our responses to problems should not be based on our emotions, but rather our trust in Him.

During the refining process, our natural responses are replaced by patience, trust, wisdom, and discernment, as we submit to God's will for our lives. Over a period of time, we slowly learn to relinquish the control of our lives to God.

God, in His great love for us, knows what it will take to dislodge all that is not of Him from our lives. In the midst of what we may consider "the good life," because things are going well for us, our lives may take a sharp U-turn. Life as we know it can change suddenly when we least expect it. We may question God, pray unceasingly, or refuse to accept our new circumstances. No amount of fighting, crying, or pleading will restore us. At such times, we must choose to trust God and submit, or to reject Him and find a solution that gives us peace of mind and a determination to go on.

Adversities test our faith. Hebrews 11:1 says, "Faith is being sure of what we hope for and certain of what we do not see." We can say we know God and know His Word, but our behavior reveals the true motivations of our heart. Others can see if our walk matches our talk, especially when we're squeezed on every side, forcing what's inside us to ooze out.

We may pretend with others, but we can never pretend with God. Others may hear our words of faith and take for granted that we are able to withstand all that comes our way. But God knows our weaknesses and our strengths. He knows whether our words are based on faith in Him or faith in ourselves.

To reveal us to ourselves, God may take away all the things we think support us. Rarely do we do as 1 Thessalonians 5:18 says: "Give thanks in all circumstances." We hurt and we want relief—immediately. When God doesn't respond, we think He has failed us. That may be our perspective of a situation, but it is not God's perspective. Isaiah 55:8 says, "My thoughts are not your thoughts, neither are your ways my ways."

Very few people like doing laundry or cleaning their house from top to bottom. Both are necessary, whether we like them or not. When God begins to turn up the heat and refine us, we should not fight Him. The blood of Jesus redeemed us from the slave market of sin, but there are still strongholds of sin in our lives. Therefore, God has to take us through the refining process to burn away the impurities, plant our feet solidly in Him, and form us into His image.

When suffering enters our lives, we are not pleased. We are like the dog who runs from his master when it's time for a bath. The dog's master knows he is smelly and needs a bath, but the dog doesn't know it. In fact, as far as the dog is concerned, the smellier the better! God sees and knows the sin areas in our lives. We may or may not see our sin. That's why we should submit to the suffering in our lives and learn from it.

Suffering makes us realize we are not in control. We can choose one of two responses to suffering—handle it our way or trust God to carry us through. If we handle it our way, we have failed the test. The area God wants to clean remains uncleaned because we would not allow Him to accomplish His work. If we trust God to carry us through the suffering He allows in our lives, His purposes for us will be accomplished.

We may try to do things our way, but in the end we are forced to do it God's way. But that doesn't mean we like it. Jonah is a great example of this. God knew his heart attitude toward the Assyrians. Therefore, He sent him to preach against Nineveh. And what was the response of Jonah, that great prophet of God? He ran the other way!

Jonah felt so comfortable with his decision that he was able to sleep on board the ship during a violent storm. The captain and sailors were afraid because the storm threatened to destroy the ship. Everyone called on their god. Jonah slept. The sailors threw the cargo in the sea to lighten the load. Jonah still slept. Then the captain went to him and said: "How can you sleep? Get up and call on your god! Maybe he will take notice of us, and we will not perish." Finally, Jonah was forced to get up.

No god responded to the dire situation of the sailors. Therefore, they decided to cast lots to see who was responsible for their calamity. Of course the lot fell on Jonah. Only when the sailors questioned him did he acknowledge his God. It is interesting that he knew what had to be done to calm the storm. When he told the sailors to throw him overboard, they refused. They showed greater kindness to Jonah, even with their lives at risk, than Jonah showed the Ninevites.

It was not until the men realized they had no control in the matter that they did what Jonah said, and then only after prayer. Jonah 1:14 gives their prayer: "O Lord, please do not let us die for taking this man's life. Do not hold us accountable for killing an innocent man, for you, O Lord, have done as you pleased."

They willingly submitted to God's will even though He was not their God. In contrast, Jonah knew God and yet fought against His will. We may be more like Jonah than we care to admit, especially when we knowingly disobey God's Word.

As Jonah sank beneath the waves, the raging water ceased. God sent a great fish to swallow Jonah. For three days, Jonah stayed in the fish. In darkness. Covered with water. Wrapped in seaweed. Forced into a situation from which he could not run. Jonah had to submit to God's refining. And so he did. From inside the belly of the fish, he remembered God and repented. God heard and responded. God commanded the fish to vomit Jonah on dry ground.

Again, Jonah received God's Word to preach to Nineveh. Jonah obeyed. Nineveh can be compared to Washington, DC. in that it was the capital of the Assyrian Empire. For three days, Jonah proclaimed God's Word. Everyone heard it, including the king. All who heard God's Word fasted and turned from their evil ways! Jonah's message had accomplished its purpose. God had compassion on the people and did not destroy them.

God's actions angered Jonah. He told God:

*O Lord, this is why I was so quick to flee to Tarshish. I knew that you are a gracious and compassionate God, slow to anger and abounding in love, a God who relents from sending calamity. Now, O Lord, take away my life, for it is better for me to die than to live (Jonah 4:2-3).*

Even though Jonah had repented and been used by God to bring salvation to the Ninevites, his heart was not right toward them. God could not release him from His refining fire. He asked Jonah: "Have you any right to be angry?" Jonah did not respond. Instead he went to a place east of the city, made himself a shelter, and waited to see what God would do.

Angry Jonah. Loving God. To give Jonah shade and ease his discomfort, God provided a vine that miraculously matured in one day. Jonah received the blessing of God and rested in its shade. Yet his heart toward the Ninevites remained unchanged.

The next day, God brought a worm which chewed the vine and caused it and its shade to wither. Then He sent a scorching east wind that caused Jonah to grow faint. Again Jonah said, "It would be better for me to die than to live" (Jonah 4:8). Jonah focused on himself during the refining process, as do we. Seldom do we realize the impact of our actions on others. We can see their sin, but we can't see our own.

Jonah told God he had a right to be angry at the vine—that he was angry enough to die. In Jonah 4:10-11 God's response to him was:

*You have been concerned about this vine, though you did not tend it or make it grow. It sprang up overnight and died overnight. But Nineveh has more than a hundred and twenty thousand people who cannot tell their right hand from their left, and many cattle as well. Should I not be concerned about that great city?*

Like Jonah, we may be so intent on what we believe is right and how we feel God should act, that we refuse to submit to His refining process in our lives. We are not afraid to challenge the God of the universe who holds our life's breath in His hands. Sometimes we are so angry with Him that death seems a better option than submission. However, death does not accomplish His purpose in our lives—submission does.

Jonah chose to do things his way, just like some of us do. Others may decide to submit to God as Esther did.

Esther, a young Jewish girl, and her uncle, Mordecai, lived in Susa, the capital of the Persian Empire. Life, as they knew it, changed when Queen Vashti refused to appear before her husband, King Xerxes, and his guests, after they had spent seven days partying and drinking. Queen Vashti was removed from her position because of her refusal to obey the king's command. All the beautiful women in the kingdom were taken into the king's harem. From them, he would choose the new queen.

Without her consent, God's plan was for Esther to become part of the king's harem. She pleased Hegai, the keeper of the harem. He immediately gave her beauty treatments, special food, personal servants, and the best room in the harem. It's amazing how God opens the eyes of others to see the value of His servants—even when we do not see our value. When God allows our testing, and we choose to submit to it, He will provide our needs during the test.

During the twelve month period of beauty treatments, Mordecai remained in contact with Esther. Daily he checked on her because she was his adopted daughter and he loved her. God gave Esther favor with all who saw her. It is no surprise that the king chose her as his new queen.

When we are in God's will, usually our actions are not offensive to others. If God has given us favor in the eyes of others, it is He who exalted us, not we ourselves. Psalm 75:7 says, "It is God who judges: He brings one down, he exalts another."

As queen, Esther enjoyed the good life. She saw the king only when he summoned her. Others cooked, cleaned, and ran her errands. She had the responsibility of looking good so that she would please the king when he summoned her. Not a bad life.

Before we start envying Esther, we should realize that God allowed her to be queen because that would be the place of her testing. Too often we may resent the position, prestige, finances, or lifestyles of others when we have no idea how God has used those very things to hone and refine them. We tend to focus on the physical and material, not the spiritual.

God allowed Mordecai to overhear two officials conspiring to assassinate the king. He told Esther about the plot, and she told the king. Esther credited Mordecai for uncovering the plot. She did not try to take credit for what she had not done. This action shows Esther's humility. It is not uncommon for some people to take credit for the work of others—and then justify their actions. This does not please God. Attitudes such as Esther's please Him because His will can be accomplished through our lives.

At this time, Mordecai's actions were not recognized and honored by the king. Sometimes we want to be recognized for our actions, especially if they are good. We want others to attach "goodness" to our name. If they don't, we may quietly simmer in resentment, vowing never to waste our time on good deeds again. That's our way, not God's. He does not give up and stop coming to our aid, regardless of the number of times we do not recognize His goodness and give Him honor. He remains faithful to us as Mordecai remained faithful to God and Esther.

A man called Haman challenged Mordecai's faithfulness to God. Because Mordecai would not bow to Haman and give him honor, Haman devised a wily plot to get rid of Mordecai: he persuaded King Xerxes to issue a decree to destroy all the Jews in the kingdom. Now remember that it was Mordecai who saved the king when he revealed a plot to assassinate him. Yet the very king whose life Mordecai saved was the one who sought his destruction and the destruction of his people. We may feel the same way at times when we feel we have done good, only to have bad things happen to us.

Mordecai fasted in sackcloth and ashes. When Esther heard about his condition, she sent him clothes, but Mordecai refused to wear them. Like Esther, we may attempt to provide topical or temporary relief in a situation without discovering and fixing the root cause of the problem. We look for a quick fix, hoping it will be sufficient. It may work temporarily, but not permanently.

Mordecai instructed Esther what to do. He told her to go into the king's presence and beg for mercy. But Esther knew that no matter how good she looked, going into his presence without being summoned could mean death. Therefore, Esther sent this reply to Mordecai's request:

*All the king's officials and the people of the royal provinces know that for any man or woman who approaches the king in the inner court without being summoned, the king has but one law: that he be put to death. The only exception to this is for the king to extend the gold scepter to him and spare his life. But thirty days have passed since I was called to go to the king (Esther 4:11).*

Esther feared for her life. God was getting ready to test her. She had to choose between God and His people or the lifestyle she had come to know and enjoy. Before her choice was made, Mordecai sent this message:

> *Do not think that because you are in the king's house you alone of all the Jews will escape. For if you remain silent at this time, relief and deliverance for the Jews will arise from another place, but you and your father's family will perish. And who knows but that you have come to royal position for such a time as this? (Esther 4:13-14)*

God places us in positions to be of service to Him. We may think He has just chosen to bless us greatly, and that we can live our lives as we please. That's not the case. God knows the future and prepares us for what's ahead. He makes sure we are where He wants us to be so He can use us when needed. We may think the price is too great for us to pay, but He doesn't. He Himself did not hesitate to send His own Son to die on the cross for our sins. We should be just as willing to do all we can to bring about His will on earth.

Esther requested that Mordecai and the Jews fast for her for three days and three nights. Afterwards, she promised to go to King Xerxes as Mordecai had instructed. She said, "When this is done, I will go to the king, even though it is against the law. And if I perish, I perish" (Esther 4:16). Esther accepted the possibility of her death.

Only when we choose to submit to God, die to self, and step out in faith will we experience the goodness of God's love. We must be wholeheartedly sold out to doing what pleases Him, whether we like it or not. Usually this causes us distress. Yet, distress can be a good thing when it loosens and dislodges fear, distrust, rebellion, or any other sin in our lives that is not pleasing to Him. We are free of the impurity that was imbedded in our lives. Faith replaces sin, and God is honored.

At the end of the three days and three nights, Esther approached the king. He extended his scepter to her, signifying his permission for her to approach him. It is amazing that, when Esther received his favor, she did not run to him and immediately share her bad news. She waited. Whether she received that strategy from God is not known. But we do know that her patience and timing led to the saving of the lives of her people, the Jews.

Like Esther, we must learn that God places us in positions of influence for His purposes, whatever they may be. We have a choice as to whether or not we will choose self-comfort and happiness, or do what is right in God's eyes. But we should know that God, not we, can bring peace in adverse circumstances, for He protects His children.

## PERSONAL APPLICATION

At the beginning of the chapter, Jackie and Rhonda discussed the attitudes of some of the people they had encountered. We have also met people who feel as though there is no need for them to change. They believe they can do as they please and still be acceptable. They do not hesitate to point out the intolerance of others, but are quick to judge others based on their own beliefs.

Whenever we enter a new phase of life, we cannot behave as before and think that others will accept it. Infantile behavior is not tolerated in elementary school. Neither is adolescent behavior accepted in the workplace. And single behavior in a mate does not meet the expectations of too many spouses. Some things belong to the past, and should stay in the past.

If that is true on the human level, why should we expect God to ignore or tolerate the sinful behavior we had before coming to Him? God is holy. Man is sinful. To become a vessel of honor, sanctified, and useful to the Master, we must choose holiness. The only way to achieve holiness is to submit to the refining fires God allows in our lives.

Accepting Jesus as our Lord and Savior cleanses us from our sin. But that is only the beginning of our walk with Him. We need to learn of Him. We get to know Him through reading the Bible and allowing the Holy Spirit to give us understanding as we meditate on the Word. This gives us the purity needed when we are tested.

Some of us may be like Jonah and have a water experience. Our rebellion against God can make us feel as though our circumstances are taking our breath away. We look around for help, but none is forthcoming. Only when we acknowledge our sin, repent, and turn to God, does He provide our way of escape. God is faithful to His Word, as He promises in Isaiah 43:2: "When you pass through the waters, I will be with you; and when you pass through the rivers, they will not sweep over you."

Although Jonah was a prophet of God, it did not prevent him from being refined. We cannot assume that God should accept us "as is" because He is holy. Ephesians 1:4 says: "For he chose us in him before the creation of the world to be holy and blameless in his sight." If He chose us to be holy, then we should submit to all He allows in our lives to refine us.

Some of us may be required to pass through the fire. Shadrach, Meshach, and Abednego did not fear King Nebuchadnezzar. When he told them to bow down to his image or be thrown in a fiery furnace, they responded:

*If we are thrown into the blazing furnace, the God we serve is able to save us from it, and he will rescue us from your hand, O king. But even if he does not, we want you to know, O king, that we will not serve your gods or worship the image of gold you have set up (Daniel 3:17-18).*

Shadrach, Meshach, and Abednego, as well as Esther, had to choose God over their very lives. God rewarded them by saving their lives. Stephen, in Acts 7, made that same decision. However, God allowed His death. When we come to the point of trusting God with our lives, we are ready to walk through the fire. We are willing to know from experience if Isaiah 43:2 is true—"When you walk through the fire, you will not be burned; the flames will not set you ablaze."

Instead of presenting ourselves to God and expecting Him to use us "as is," we learn to depend on Him to carry us during the refinement process. We trust that He will allow only what is necessary to burn the impurities from our lives so we can be holy as He is holy. That is how He conforms us into the image of His Son.

# CHAPTER SEVEN

# Surrendering to God

## Surrender

Jesse sat at his desk and glanced at the clock. 6:00 A.M. He took his laptop from the carrying case, opened it, and then closed it. He then opened the bottom drawer of his mahogany desk, took out his Bible, and placed it on top of the laptop. Then he closed his eyes and bowed his head.

*"Thank You, Lord, for all You are allowing in my life—for giving me the opportunity to suffer for You. You know me better than I know myself. Therefore, please continue to refine me and strip away everything in my life that is not pleasing to You.*

*"Father, my desire is to be like You. Help me to focus on Your sovereignty and power, instead of pitying myself and doubting Your control. I know that You have my best interests at heart, even though I do not always act like it. Sometimes it's hard for me to accept difficulties when I think I don't deserve them.*

*"Lord, teach me that Your ways are not my ways and that Your thoughts are not my thoughts. Help me to*

understand that You have eternity in view, not just my present situation. Help me to take my focus off my feelings, and focus instead on accomplishing Your will in my life—without crying and complaining.

"Teach me how to truly trust You. At times, when things are going well, I think that there is not a problem in my life. But when I'm tested, I realize that my faith is not as strong as I think it is. My faith seems to go up and down like a yo-yo before coming to rest firmly in You. I try to tell myself that "all things work together for good" but Lord, sometimes my emotions overrule my will. I want to be a living sacrifice, but that does not always happen.

"Lord, You know I want to die to self and learn to intercede for others. When I think I've reached that point, something always happens to let me know I've fallen short of that goal. I tend to be short when someone challenges my patience or is the exact opposite of my personality, and I do not always pray for them as I should.

"If I feel others are unfairly criticizing me or persecuting me without cause, my response does not necessarily remind them that I belong to you. I lapse into my old ways and respond in ways that are not appropriate. Help me, Lord. Do whatever it takes to make me more like You—for my desire is to be conformed to Your image.

"Loving You and accepting all You allow in my life stretches me. I thought it would be easy, but it's not. If it were just You and me, there wouldn't be a problem. However, when You use others who behave poorly to accomplish my refining, I'm tempted to reject what You are teaching me.

"Father, it is time for me to grow up spiritually. Help me to accept and embrace all You allow in my life, and teach me how to be a good witness to others as I intercede on their behalves. Let them see You in me, not me. Teach me to encourage and help those You allow to cross my path. Use me Father because I want to be greatly used by You.

*I'm ready and willing to become Your ambassador in all
I do and say."*

---

## SURRENDER BASED ON LOVE

One of Webster's definitions of surrender is "to give (oneself) over to a passion, influence, etc." We give ourselves to our children, our careers, our spouses, our friends, or whatever we love, without giving a second thought about it. Whenever they need us, we are there for them, regardless of personal cost.

That should be our attitude when we choose to surrender to God. If we love Him, we should give Him our best. We cannot be co-leaders with God. Either He is in control of our lives or we are in control. Unless we are willing to obey God and submit to His will for our lives, we have not surrendered to Him.

Love for God is not based on our feelings. *Vine's Complete Expository Dictionary of Old and New Testament Words* says: "Christian love has God for its primary object, and expresses itself first of all in implicit obedience to His commandments. Self will, that is, self-pleasing, is the negation of love to God."

We gladly surrender to what we love. In fact, everything we do is to please the person we love. If we love ourselves most, all our actions will be to please ourselves, and no one else. We obtain a job so we can make money to do the things we desire. We develop relationships so others can help us accomplish our needs. We schedule our time to reflect our interests and desires. We are the center of our lives, and our choices reflect it.

An example of this type of self love, or a will to please self, can be witnessed in marriage. Regardless of the number of years together, spouses who love themselves more than their mates will place themselves first. Whatever interests them is what they will pursue—not the interests of their spouses or families. If challenged, they will justify their actions or place the blame on others. Rarely do they acknowledge they are at fault. As long as their goals are achieved, they are satisfied.

"Why shouldn't I enjoy myself?" asked Frank. "Don't I provide a good quality of life for you and the family?"

"This is not about your ability to provide for us. I'm asking you to spend time with me—apart from functions with others. Why can't we schedule time to be alone? Is that so difficult?" countered Liz.

"We are alone every night. I work hard. Why shouldn't I be able to do the things I like?"

"Frank, our relationship is not solely based on fulfilling your needs. When we married, we became one but you still act as though you are single. How can you love me if you aren't willing to spend time with me? What sacrifices are you willing to make for our relationship?"

"Sacrifices? What has that got to do with anything? I take care of my responsibilities so why can't I have alone time?"

As long as the spouses who love themselves are getting their needs met, these unhealthy relationships can continue. Not until they choose to surrender to God and place Him in the center of their lives will they be able to love others as they should. No one can serve two masters. We must choose whom we will serve—God or ourselves. When we choose to serve God, we finally have real satisfaction, true peace, and new direction in our lives.

When God is the center of our lives, we gladly attempt to put Him first. All our actions are geared to please Him. Our love for Him grows more and more as we choose to obey His commands. We trust Him to provide our needs and keep us safe. Our desire is to lift Him up and give Him the glory, not draw attention to ourselves or what we can do.

Our love for God must be a choice of the will, not feelings. We may not always feel like we love God, especially when He allows something in our lives that we do not like or want. But we should not withdraw or withhold our love from Him based on circumstances. If God is the center of our lives, we are in a right relationship with Him.

Paul uses marriage as an illustration of Jesus' relationship to the Church. Ephesians 5:25-32 says:

*Husbands, love your wives, just as Christ loved the church and gave himself up for her to make her holy, cleansing her by the washing with water through the word, and to present her to himself as a radiant church, without stain or wrinkle or any other blemish, but holy and blameless. In this same way, husbands ought to love their wives as their own bodies. He who loves his wife loves himself. After all, no one ever hated his own body, but he feeds and cares for it, just as Christ does the church—for we are members of his body. For this reason a man will leave his father and mother and be united to his wife, and the two will become one flesh. This is a profound mystery—but I am talking about Christ and the church.*

In Scripture only two allowances are given for ending marriage—death and adultery. When we die, we end our earthly relationship with God and enter into our heavenly relationship with Him. Surely we wouldn't complain about that. However, an adulterous relationship means we have given God's position in our lives to another person. The relationship we once had no longer exists.

The book of Hosea describes an adulterous marriage. Hosea's wife, Gomer, put her needs first. She did not care how her actions affected, humiliated, or hurt Hosea emotionally as long as her needs were met. She pursued her lovers even though it destroyed her relationship with Hosea. She valued herself, not Hosea.

Scripture does not tell us of Hosea's affections toward Gomer, but it does tell us of his love for God. When God told Hosea to reconcile with Gomer, he did. Hosea did not object or tell God about his personal pain in his marriage. Instead, he chose to obey God and stay in the relationship with his wife, rather than take the escape the Law provided. Hosea's love for God led him to put God first and obey Him.

Only when we love God wholeheartedly can we put Him first and obey His commands, especially in difficult circumstances. It is a choice of our will, not our emotions. This kind of love represents God's love for us. It is *agapé* love. Vine's says:

> In respect of *agapao* as used of God, it expresses the deep and constant love and interest of a perfect Being towards entirely unworthy objects, producing and fostering a reverential love in them towards the Giver, and a practical love towards those who are partakers of the same, and a desire to help others to seek the Giver.

Constant love. That doesn't seem to have anything to do with our feelings, but it describes the type of love we desire from others. Maybe we should recognize that others are like us, incapable of such a deep and constant love. Therefore, we should not ask them to do only what God is capable of doing in our lives—loving us deeply and constantly regardless of our actions.

## TRUST

We've either said or heard others say, "Trust me." Our definition of trust may not be the same as Webster's, which says trust is: "a confident reliance on the integrity, veracity, or justice of another."

We don't have a problem with trust as long as we are not disappointed or deceived. Usually, we are willing to overlook something once. However, if someone continuously disappoints us, we may become angry and no longer trust him or her. When that happens, we are leery of giving others our trust—even putting trust in God. We assume He will treat us as everyone else has. Therefore, He has to prove Himself over and over to us before we finally have enough faith in Him to surrender to His will for our lives.

In the book of Judges, Gideon had a problem trusting God. When the angel of the LORD appeared to him and said, "The LORD is with you, mighty warrior," Gideon was not impressed.

> *"But sir," Gideon replied, "if the LORD is with us, why has all this happened to us? Where are all his wonders that our*

*fathers told us about when they said, 'Did not the LORD
bring us up out of Egypt?' But now the LORD has abandoned
us and put us into the hand of Midian" (Judges 6:13).*

God spoke. Gideon questioned. God affirmed His faithfulness.
Gideon doubted. God waited for Gideon to prepare and offer his
sacrifice. Gideon feared. God comforted. Gideon obeyed. God
commanded. Gideon asked for a sign. God responded. Gideon
asked for another sign. Again God responded. Finally, Gideon
obeyed God's commands.

We are no different than Gideon when we believe God has not
done as He promised. We become angry and pout. Our hearts
become hard and, unless we see God's faithfulness, we hesitate to
follow and obey Him.

The Apostle Peter also doubted God even though he had walked
with Jesus and witnessed His miracles. One amazing night, he had
even trusted Jesus' word, gotten out of the boat, and walked on water
to meet Him. But the miracle of walking on water was short lived
because the moment Peter took his eyes off Jesus, he sunk.

Peter's temporary failure did not render him useless to God. He
continued walking with Jesus and growing in his relationship with
Him. Yet, the three years he spent with Jesus did not prevent him
from denying he knew Him. After Jesus had risen from the grave,
He restored Peter. Even though Peter had a difficult time forgiving
himself, God did not. We, like Gideon and Peter, may doubt God
but our doubts do not prevent God from using us.

## FAITH

We must understand the distinction between faith in man and
faith in God. *Vine's Complete Expository Dictionary of Old and New
Testament Words* lists the three main elements of faith in God as:
"(1) A firm conviction, producing a full acknowledgment of God's
revelation or truth; (2) A personal surrender to Him; and (3) A
conduct inspired by such surrender."

Faith in God frees us from making backup plans. If our trust is
in Him instead of ourselves, we know He is sufficient to provide all

our needs when trials arise. In fact, trials can be viewed as opportunities to strengthen or increase our faith in God. If we shrink back from following Him, or depending on Him because of difficult times in our lives, then our faith is not as great as we think. When we believe God is greater than anything He allows in our lives, we do not hesitate to turn to Him. The only way we are prepared for this kind of faith is through having a personal relationship with God. We develop this relationship through salvation, prayer, reading the Bible, and fellowship with other believers.

Once we have fully surrendered to God, we know without a doubt that His Word is true. We can expect Him to do exactly what He says, according to His plan, and in His timing. Nothing can shake our confidence in Him, for we are one with Him in spirit since His Holy Spirit indwells us.

Our spiritual connection with God opens the door for us to surrender to Him. As new believers we are not fully surrendered to Him. When babies are learning to walk, they take one step at a time. Sometimes they fall, but as they become more confident they are able to walk further. As we practice our walk with God, surrendering to Him helps us become a vessel of honor, sanctified, useful to the Master. He can use us as He chooses without our fighting against Him.

When we are fully surrendered to God, our responses to circumstances change. We no longer complain and ask God why He allows certain things in our lives. We agree with Romans 8:28 which says, "We know that in all things God works for the good of those who love him, who have been called according to his purpose." Instead of doubting, we choose to trust and believe that God is in control, even though it may not be our idea of control. In this way, our conduct will please Him, and our talk will match our walk. We cannot proclaim God's Word to the world and yet not allow it to see our different response to difficulties. Either God is faithful, just as we say, or He isn't. There's no middle ground.

Scripture says, "The righteous will live by faith." To emphasize the importance of this principle, God records it four times in Scripture: Habakkuk 2:4, Romans 1:17, Galatians 3:11, and Hebrews 10:38.

Paul says that righteousness is from God (Philippians 3:9). When we are surrendered to Him, He is the One who teaches us how to respond with righteous behavior. Not only does He sustain and guide us during difficult times, but He also teaches us the right things to do. What an awesome God we serve!

## FELLOWSHIP

When we know God and are known by Him, we are walking in the light rather than darkness. 1 John 1:5-7 says:

*God is light; in him there is no darkness at all. If we claim*
*to have fellowship with him yet walk in the darkness, we lie*
*and do not live by the truth. But if we walk in the light, as*
*he is in the light, we have fellowship with one another, and*
*the blood of Jesus, his Son, purifies us from all sin.*

Then sin no longer controls our lives or hearts. God is in control. We can freely communicate with Him and enter His presence in prayer. We have a direct route to intercede for others and to pray for ourselves. When God opens the door of fellowship to us, only we can close it by sinning. Yet, please know that our fellowship with God is not terminated because of sin. First John 1:9 says, "If we confess our sins, he is faithful and just and will forgive us our sins and purify us from all unrighteousness." Whenever we fall or stumble, God has already provided the solution. We only need to apply the answer He has provided and our fellowship with Him is restored. When our spouses, children, families, or friends ask forgiveness, we should not continue to hold grudges. As God forgives us, we should willingly choose to forgive others. That's one way we can show others how God indwells us.

## PERSONAL APPLICATION

The prayer at the beginning of the chapter represents a person struggling with a relationship with God. Surrendering to Him is not instantaneous. Jacob wrestled with God in Genesis 32. It was not until later, when God changed his name to Israel that his struggle ended. Jacob set up a pillar and anointed it in the place of his communion with God, Bethel, and then moved on. Jacob's surrender to God allowed him to face the other difficulties that occurred in his life.

God has not changed. He desires that we surrender to Him so we can discover His great love for us. It is only when we learn of His faithfulness in our difficult situations that we can trust Him in other areas of our lives. We are no longer controlled and bound by worries or stress. Matthew 11:28-30 says:

> *Come to me, all you who are weary and burdened, and I will give you rest. Take my yoke upon you and learn from me, for I am gentle and humble in heart, and you will find rest for your souls. For my yoke is easy and my burden is light.*

What a great promise! What better way to come to know and love God. When we cease our struggle with Him, we can experience His goodness and love. We learn that His yoke is easy and His burden is light. Our attitudes and actions reflect our joy of being living sacrifices for Him. We strive to be holy and pleasing to God. Romans 12:1-2 says:

> *Therefore, I urge you, brothers, in view of God's mercy, to offer your bodies as living sacrifices, holy and pleasing to God—this is your spiritual act of worship. Do not conform any longer to the pattern of this world, but be transformed by the renewing of your mind. Then you will be able to test and approve what God's will is—his good, pleasing and perfect will.*

We are transformed by obeying God instead of satisfying our personal desires. Obedience to His Word and His will for our lives allows us to be molded into His image. Our first desire is to please Him in all we do and say. This is the ultimate goal of godly surrender.

# CHAPTER EIGHT

## *Going for the Gold*

*Your faith—of greater worth than gold.*
1 Peter 1:7

What can I do? I'm tired of waiting for Charles to love me. Even though I'm married, it's as though I'm single because I'm still alone. I know I'm supposed to trust God, and I have. But for years, I have waited patiently for God to change my husband's heart and He hasn't. Nothing has changed in my marriage," said Kathy.

"You've changed. You are not the person you were ten years ago," said Tiffany.

"I know I've changed. That's not my question. I want to know when my husband will change. Every year I keep hoping that God will work in Kevin's heart, but He doesn't."

"Remember when Peter asked Jesus about John's future, Jesus basically told him it was none of his business. That Peter's job was to follow Him."

"Tiff, I don't want to hear what Scripture says. I want an answer."

"Kathy, I am giving you an answer. Let God do His own work. You are responsible for yourself only."

"Don't you think I deserve to be happy?"

"Kathy, happiness is dependent on circumstances, and your circumstances aren't happy. But do you have peace?"

"Yes."

"What about joy, comfort, and security in God."

"Tiffany, I have all those things. I just want a husband who can share my spiritual blessings. I want someone who knows and loves God because He will then know how to love me."

"Kathy, that's what every married woman wants. Before God can give us the desires of our hearts, He has to prepare us. Look at the changes you have made in the last ten years. If God had given you your heart's desire ten years ago, you wouldn't have been ready for it."

"I know, but what about now? I'm ready now."

"I'm not God. I can't give you the answer you want to hear. But I do know that God is faithful. His will will be done, in His timing, and in His way. Continue to follow and obey Him. He has not forgotten or forsaken you."

"I know. It's just that I get so tired of waiting sometimes."

"I understand—just don't give up on your husband. God is aware of your situation. Just as He has strengthened you in the past, He will continue to strengthen you in the future. Trust Him to meet your needs in ways you cannot imagine."

---

James 5:16 tells us that the prayer of a righteous person is powerful and effective. Armed with that knowledge, those purified by God are not hesitant to use their spiritual weapons. They stand strong because they know the Lord and His power. They realize that Satan uses people and circumstances to bring about opposition and confusion in their lives. Daily, they must rely on the armor of God found in Ephesians 6: 10-18—truth, righteousness, the gospel of peace, faith, the Word of God, and prayer. Rarely do they seek to accomplish God's will in their own power.

Those who have reached this point spiritually, have learned that God uses adversity in their lives to strengthen and develop them. No longer are they complaining or fighting against Him because they know He loves them and desires to conform them into His image. But that does not mean a strong Christian will never doubt. Even though John the Baptist proclaimed Jesus as the Messiah, baptized Him, and saw the Spirit come down from heaven and rest on Him, he sent his disciples to ask Jesus, "Are you the one who was to come, or should we expect someone else?" (Matthew 11:2).

Jesus was not surprised or hurt by John's question. Instead He said, "I tell you the truth: Among those born of women there has not risen anyone greater than John the Baptist; yet he who is least in the kingdom of heaven is greater than he" (Matthew 11:11).

Sometimes we may be tempted to believe that we are fighting the battle alone. That is not the case. When we are battle weary, we tend to believe only what we can see. This is what happened to Elijah in 1 Kings 19:1-4. Despite the magnificent miracle that had occurred on Mt. Carmel, Elijah became frightened when he heard Jezebel's threat. He ran for his life and wished that he was dead. But God met him at his low point and provided.

Our feelings do not dictate God's response to us. We may believe He doesn't care for us, or has forgotten about us, because He does not move according to our time schedule. But God is faithful. He knows what we can bear. Whenever we are tempted to act in a way that is not according to His will, He will provide a plan of escape according to 1 Corinthians 10:13:

> *No temptation has seized you except what is common to man. And God is faithful; he will not let you be tempted beyond what you can bear. But when you are tempted, he will also provide a way out so that you can stand up under it.*

We should not be bound by sight. Physical sight allows us to be aware of our surroundings. It should not be the measure of our trust in God. Second Corinthians 5:7 tells us: "We live by faith, not by sight." Therefore, what we see should not determine our obedience to God or our walk with Him.

Elisha, God's companion for Elijah, asked Elijah for a double portion of his spirit (2 Kings 2:9). God granted Elisha's request, and he performed many miracles. When Elisha realized God's faithfulness to him, he was not bound by physical sight anymore.

When the Aramean king sent his army to capture Elisha, he was not afraid because he trusted in God's provision. However, Elisha's servant lacked spiritual sight. After the city had been surrounded, he said to his master, "Oh, my lord, what shall we do?" Second Kings 6:16-17 records Elisha's response:

> *"Don't be afraid," the prophet answered. "Those who are with us are more than those who are with them." And Elisha prayed, "O Lord, open his eyes so he may see." Then the Lord opened the servant's eyes, and he looked and saw the hills full of horses and chariots of fire all around Elisha.*

As long as our eyes are closed spiritually, we are not in tune with God's work in our lives. We rely on self instead of Him. Some of us may act like Moses. When he saw an Egyptian beating a Hebrew, he looked around to make sure no one was looking before killing the man (Exodus 2:12). However, others witnessed his actions.

Our actions are also witnessed by others—not always on earth but certainly in heaven. Whether we like it or not, everything we do is visible to God. He knows whether we are living by faith or by sight.

## COMMITTED AND DISCIPLINED

When we come to God as clay vessels, we may not be very committed or disciplined in our walk with Him. As we read His Word and persevere during trials in our lives, we become more and more committed and disciplined. In fact, by the time He is ready to use us as golden vessels, He can count on us because we have been trustworthy and faithful servants in the past.

Spiritual growth occurs as we persevere in our walk with God. Salvation is the beginning, not the end of our journey. Our acceptance of Jesus Christ as our Lord and Savior makes us clay vessels.

God begins the molding process that transforms us into His image. If our commitment to Him is not sincere, as soon as trials begin, we will fall away. Clay vessels, not grounded in Christ, cannot endure the heat that is required to refine them.

Wooden vessels are those who desire to know more about the God they love. They desire to have God's Word etched on their hearts. Whenever they have the opportunity to read or study God's Word, they do. It is at this stage that they begin to fall in love with God. The more they learn about Him, the more they want to know because they are caught up in His goodness, love, and mercy. Mercy is important to them because they realize they could never have approached a holy God without the shed blood of Christ.

Silver vessels are those who are growing in their commitment to God. They have accepted Christ and regularly make time to know God through reading and studying His Word and attending church with fellow believers. Their foundation of faith is laid, but now it must be tested with God's refining fire. Trials strengthen the faith of silver vessels. Anything in them that is not of God will surface in the heat of battle. If they choose to hold onto their impurities, the trials become greater. If they choose to let go of the impurities and submit to God, they are ready to be used by Him.

Golden vessels are those who have not turned from following God. It does not mean that they have not complained or sinned along the way, it only means that they would rather walk with God than spend time with those who don't know Him. During each stage God can use His people, but golden vessels can be great encouragers to those who are still being molded or refined. Golden vessels can also share God's Word in ways that others will understand—speaking encouraging words to strengthen fellow believers.

An invaluable asset of golden vessels is prayer. Throughout Scripture, God has heard and answered the prayers of those who belong to Him. James 5:16 says: "The prayer of a righteous man is powerful and effective." Golden vessels believe that God is in control whether they can see it at the moment or not. Their faith is in Him, not themselves. Therefore, they are constantly seeking God's will regarding their lives, rather than trusting circumstances. Golden vessels are committed to walking with God, listening to Him, and obeying Him.

Once we are truly committed to God and have experienced His faithfulness to us, our visual sight does not dictate our responses to God. Instead we believe that God, who we cannot see, is in control even if it doesn't seem like it. First John 4:4 says, "You, dear children, are from God and have overcome them, because the one who is in you is greater than the one who is in the world." Golden vessels base their lives on the truth of this statement.

We must continue to trust God during difficult circumstances. We cannot turn back or give up, or we will miss the reward that awaits us at the end of our test. James 1:2-4 says:

> Consider it pure joy, my brothers, whenever you face trials of many kinds, because you know that the testing of your faith develops perseverance. Perseverance must finish its work so that you may be mature and complete, not lacking anything.

## GODLINESS

Believers who have matured in Christ and are ready to be used as golden vessels are well pleasing to God. Their desire is to know, love, and serve Him. However, this does not mean that they do not sin. It only means that when they sin, they confess their sins. Confession does not eliminate consequences, but it does bring believers back into a right relationship with God.

King David is an excellent example of this. He loved God. In fact, he is known as a man after God's heart. He was chosen by God, anointed by Samuel, and loved by the people. He has encouraged thousands with his words recorded in the Psalms. King David had it all, but that did not insulate him from sin.

When oppressed by King Saul, David refused to touch God's anointed even though others encouraged him to do so. He refused to allow other people's opinions to cause him to dishonor God. Nor did he desire the death of his son, Absalom, even when Absalom almost succeeded in stealing his kingdom. David did not allow painful circumstances outside of himself, or struggles within, to dictate his responses. He continued to trust God.

Only when David chose not to do the job God gave him did he fall into sin. Second Samuel 11:1 says, "In the spring, at the time when kings go off to war, David sent Joab out with the king's men and the whole Israelite army." David delegated his work to another instead of doing it himself. David, not God, set up the circumstances that led to his sin. We are no different from David when we choose to please ourselves instead of God.

Second Samuel 11:2-3 says:

*One evening David got up from his bed and walked around on the roof of the palace. From the roof he saw a woman bathing. The woman was very beautiful, and David sent someone to find out about her.*

It seems that David had more free time when his men and army were not around. Therefore, he could do things that he may not have done normally. He did not sin when he walked around the palace roof. He did not sin when he saw the woman bathing. However, he did sin when he refused to turn his gaze from the woman. Her beauty enticed him and tempted him to pursue a relationship with her.

Although David had wives and concubines to satisfy his sexual needs, he chose to sleep with the wife of a man serving in his army. The woman became pregnant and told David. Instead of acknowledging and confessing his sin, David sought to cover it. He sent a message to the battlefield for her husband to come home.

When Uriah, the woman's husband, arrived, David asked him about the men and the status of the battle. After a pleasant chat, David sent him home. But, unbeknownst to David, Uriah slept at the palace entrance with David's servants. When David discovered that he did not go home, he asked him why. Second Samuel 11:11 gives Uriah's answer:

*The ark and Israel and Judah are staying in tents, and my
master Joab and my lord's men are camped in the open fields.
How could I go to my house to eat and drink and lie with my
wife? As surely as you live, I will not do such a thing!*

Uriah's integrity was not influenced by David's words or gifts.
He remained faithful to what he believed. But Uriah's words did not
have a positive effect on David. Rather than admit the truth to
Uriah, David sought to undermine Uriah's decision by getting him
drunk. Still, Uriah did not sleep with his wife.

Second Samuel 11:14-15 gives David's final resolution for the
problem:

*In the morning David wrote a letter to Joab and sent it with
Uriah. In it he wrote, "Put Uriah in the front line where the
fighting is fiercest. Then withdraw from him so he will be
struck down and die."*

Joab did as instructed, and Uriah was killed. After Bathsheba,
Uriah's wife, finished mourning for her husband, David made her
his wife. Second Samuel 11:27 says: "But the thing David had done
displeased the LORD."

Just like David, we may involve others in our sin and cause
them to sin. This is not pleasing to God. When we sin, we should
not ask others to cover for us. Our desire should be to do what is
right in God's sight and encourage others to do what is pleasing to
God—not what is pleasing to us. Godly friends do not encourage
or enable their friends to sin.

God may use us greatly at one time or another, but that does
not mean we are incapable of sinning. As long as we are focused on
Him and doing the work He has given us, we will remain pleasing
to God. But when we take our eyes off Him and do the things which
please us, we open the door for sin. What we did before does not
matter. Just as the food we ate yesterday does not satisfy our present hunger, neither does previous work for God substitute for our
present actions. Daily, we must choose to obey and honor Him.

David did not show any signs of repentance until God sent His prophet Nathan to confront him. God's scathing words to David in 2 Samuel 12:7-10 were:

*I anointed you king over Israel, and I delivered you from the hand of Saul. I gave your master's house to you, and your master's wives into your arms. I gave you the house of Israel and Judah. And if all this had been too little, I would have given you even more. Why did you despise the word of the Lord by doing what is evil in his eyes? You struck down Uriah the Hittite with the sword and took his wife to be your own. You killed him with the sword of the Ammonites. Now, therefore, the sword will never depart from your house, because you despised me and took the wife of Uriah the Hittite to be your own.*

We don't get away with sin. It may seem like we have outwitted God and have escaped the consequences of our sin, but that is never the case—especially if we are gold vessels for God. He cannot allow us to do as we please if we are in His service.

David acknowledged his sin and did not complain that the consequences were too great. He accepted what God caused to happen in his life because of his sin. When we sin, we should not complain when suffering the consequences. God is fair and just. If we are to be vessels of honor, sanctified, useful to the Master, all our actions must reveal our faith in Him.

## INTERCESSION

Psalm 51:1-6 records David's prayer to God after Nathan confronted him about his sin with Bathsheba.

*Have mercy on me, O God, according to your unfailing love;*
*According to your great compassion blot out my transgressions.*
*Wash away all my iniquity and cleanse me from my sin.*
*For I know my transgressions, and my sin is always before me.*

*Against you, you only, have I sinned and done what is evil
in your sight,
So that you are proved right when you speak and justified
when you judge.
Surely you desire truth in the inner parts; you teach me wisdom in the inmost place.*

As David poured out his heart in prayer to God, so should we.
Just as David knew his transgressions, so do we know ours, especially when we have willfully sinned. There is only one cure for sin,
and that is confession. Sometimes we choose to deceive ourselves
and try to pretend that good works, gifts of money, or having self-
contempt will absolve us of sin. They don't. God has provided only
one way to cleanse sin. Until we confess to Him and accept His forgiveness, we are not in His will.

David acknowledged that God was justified in His actions. Yet,
few of us tell God that He is justified when we are suffering the consequences of our actions. When we grumble and complain while
reaping the consequences of our sin, we give others the impression
that God is not justified in His actions toward us.

What's worse is when we try to "fix things," instead of allowing
our spouses, children, families, or friends to suffer the consequences of their actions. We would rather hide their sin so others
will think well of them. What does that teach them about God?
They will believe He tolerates their sin as we tolerate it, but He
doesn't.

Overlooking or pretending that the sins of our children or family members are not worthy of God's judgment is not supported by
Scripture. Just because we tolerate their sin does not mean God
will. He is a holy God who will not lower His standards to accommodate sin. The Bible tells us what is acceptable to Him, and unless
we do what is acceptable to Him, we will not enter His presence.

Whenever gardening or farming, whatever is planted is what
will be produced. An apple seed produces an apple tree. Apple trees
usually bear more than one apple. An orange seed produces an
orange tree which bears oranges. Apple seeds do not produce

orange trees. That rule cannot be changed. If we live a life of sin then we should not be surprised with the sinful fruit we bear. Nor should we be surprised when we reap more sin than we planted. We will reap what we sow—more than we sow.

We cannot stop the sinful seeds planted by our husbands, wives, children, siblings, or family members from bearing fruit—just as we can't stop the sun from shining or the seasons from changing. This rule is applicable to every person on earth. Our job is to understand it and teach it to our loved ones so they will know whatever seeds they plant are the type of fruit that will be produced in their lives. Hosea 8:7 confirms this when it says: "Sow the wind, and reap the whirlwind."

First Peter 4:17 says, "Judgment begins with the family of God; and if it begins with us, what will the outcome be for those who do not obey the gospel of God?" As God judges us, He will judge others. Therefore, we should not try to prevent their suffering for sin, but try to help them repent and accept the consequences. How do we know that their suffering will not lead to repentance? Instead of interfering in God's work, we should intercede for those who are bound by sin, praying God's mercy on them.

Intercession, seeking God on behalf of others, is a free gift we give them. Praying for others is as important as praying for ourselves. When we have fellowship with God, we have His ear. No one can stop us from praying. There is no set formula or pattern. All that is necessary is that we share the burdens or desires of our hearts. God hears us. In His timing and in His way, He responds.

While intercession is important, remember that when it is within our ability to help others, we should do so. First John 3:17 says, "If anyone has material possessions and sees his brother in need but has not pity on him, how can the love of God be in him?" Prayer is important, but so is helping others.

## SOMETHING DIFFERENT

When we have been in God's presence, others should notice a difference in us. Moses was unaware of his radiant face after he had been in God's presence, but others noticed. They were afraid to come near him. Only when he called to them, did they draw near. Like Moses, we have the opportunity to enter God's presence.

When Jesus died on the cross, the curtain in the temple that separated the Holy Place from the Most Holy Place was torn in two from top to bottom. Since the curtain was made of strongly twisted linen and was about the width of a hand, it could not have been torn by human hands. God, not man, tore it. Therefore, no longer do we need to be represented by others to God. We have been freed by Christ to enter into His presence.

God is holy. Sin cannot stand in His presence. If we cling to our old ways, we cannot stand before God. When we submit to Him and surrender our wills to His, then He is ready to use us greatly. Others cannot help but notice the change in our lives because our responses to people, life, and circumstances are not the same. Our faces may even shine with the joy of the knowledge of His presence.

As we mature from clay to wood to silver and finally to golden vessels, our lives should reflect more and more of God's light. We mature as we obey God. We cannot obey Him if we don't know Him. The only way to know God is through accepting Jesus Christ as our Lord and Savior. We are then sealed by the Holy Spirit, who makes the Bible alive and meaningful to us. As we approach God in prayer, we are not afraid. Waiting and listening for His response, obeying Him, and walking with Him daily gives us inner peace. Gradually, we learn to put God first so that our desire is to please Him instead of ourselves. He increases, we decrease. Self-satisfaction no longer controls our lives.

We cannot have it both ways; either we reflect Him or ourselves. Becoming vessels of honor, sanctified, and useful to the Master allows others to see a difference in us. They may or may not change their behavior around us, but that is okay. Yet we must continue to live a life that is pleasing to God, regardless of what others around us do.

Without our speaking a word to those whose behavior is different from ours, God can use our mere presence to condemn their lifestyles. Second Corinthians 2:15-16 says, "For we are to God the aroma of Christ among those who are being saved and those who are perishing. To the one we are the smell of death; to the other, the fragrance of life." He, not we, condemns.

Second Corinthians 3:18 says, "And we, who with unveiled faces all reflect the Lord's glory, are being transformed into his likeness with ever-increasing glory." Do not hide or cover God's work, allow it to shine in your life. Others need to see His glory and know Him.

## PERSONAL APPLICATION

At the beginning of the chapter, Kathy was tempted to give up because she could not see a difference in her marriage. She thought that God's progress after ten years of waiting was insufficient, and she wanted more. Only when talking with Tiffany did she realize God's work in her life. Tiffany's encouragement gave her the proper perspective toward her situation.

> *Do not lose heart. Though outwardly we are wasting away,*
> *yet inwardly we are being renewed day by day. For our light*
> *and momentary troubles are achieving for us an eternal glory*
> *that far outweighs them all. So we fix our eyes not on what is*
> *seen, but on what is unseen. For what is seen is temporary,*
> *but what is unseen is eternal (2 Corinthians 4:16-18).*

Troubles often cause us to turn to God. If we trust Him to take care of us, He will take the clay vessels that we are and refine us until we reflect His glory. Believers in Jesus Christ are not focused on the temporary but on the eternal. As we grow in our relationship with God, we too should focus on the eternal. We are God's people, members of His household, and should not be discouraged by what happens on earth. We should be saying, "Thy kingdom come!"

As the world knows those who belong to it, so should God's people know those who belong to Him. Our lives should make a difference in the world because He has made a difference in us.

# CHAPTER NINE

# They Chose to Serve

*Now faith is being sure of what we hope for and certain of
what we do not see.*

Hebrews 11:1

I love sitting on your porch watching the cows graze. They seem so contented. I always feel so peaceful when I'm here. It's so relaxing—nothing like life in the city. Have you always lived in the country, Grandma?"

"Yes, baby. I've visited Houston, Dallas, Austin, San Antonio, and other places in Texas, but I love Bellville best. This is where I was born and raised."

"I can't imagine what life must have been like for you, especially in 'the olden days.' Did you have many hardships and struggles?"

"Hardships and struggles? They come with life. It doesn't matter where you live," said Grandma. "I was born in 1903, I guess that's what you mean when you say 'the olden days.' Things were different then. What you young people take for granted, we had to work hard for. But with God, nothing is impossible."

"Grandma, I know about slavery and prejudice, but what about you? Did you enjoy life and have fun?"

"Baby, I did have fun, and I'm still having fun. I enjoy serving the Lord! He's so good to me. If you're asking if there was a time when I didn't serve Him, there was. I wanted to be like my friends and do the things they did. I heard God calling, but I ignored Him."

"What happened?"

"Baby, what usually happens when people are disobedient to God? They do what they choose, and that's exactly what I did. I thought I knew God, but I didn't. Even though I went to church, I did the things I wanted to do instead of the things God wanted me to do. That's when I received my first real spanking from God, and it was a good one. That's what I needed to repent and turn me to God, but this time I obeyed Him instead of pretending to obey Him. Even though I had to wear the same dress every week to church, I was grateful to be there. From that day to this one, I have tried to obey God in all I do."

"Grandma, did you ever get tired of being married? Men can be so stubborn at times. Sometimes I'm happy to be married, and other times I wonder if I married the right person."

"The longer you live, you'll discover that men are like horses. Each one has a different stride. You can't change the stride, but you can learn how to walk in harmony regardless of the stride."

"I never thought of it like that. What about your children? How did you raise them and teach them about God?"

"Proverbs 22:6 tells parents to train a child in the way he should go, and when he is old he will not turn from it. I believed those words when I had my first child, and I believe them now. Nowadays, young parents expose their children to things they should not see or know because they are too young to handle it."

"Such as?"

"Look at the television shows or the video games children are allowed to play. They see too much sex and violence. How can they know what's right or wrong if they are not taught? When my children were babies, I taught them about God. Of course, it was in a way they could understand. As they got older, I expected more from them because they knew right from wrong. I tried not to shield them from the consequences of their actions after they had been warned what would happen."

"Grandma, motherhood is more demanding today. Most moms work outside the home and do not always have the time to supervise what their children watch on TV or monitor the video games they play. But that doesn't mean they don't love their children."

"Baby, God loves us, but He has warned us what will happen if we do certain things. How do you expect children to obey and respect you if they can do as they please?"

"Grandma, they will know the difference between right and wrong. They're not dumb."

"How will they know if they are not taught?"

## PEOPLE WHO MAKE A DIFFERENCE

"Faith is being sure of what we hope for and certain of what we do not see" (Hebrews 11:1). When we are young, we base our beliefs on what we see. That is not faith. However, when we are born again—believe Jesus died for our sin and accept Him as our Savior and Lord—our spiritual eyes are opened because the Holy Spirit lives within us. We have the capacity to see the world as God does. What pleases God should please us. What offends Him should offend us because we are one with Him spiritually.

Hebrews 11 gives a partial listing of those in God's "Hall of Faith." Abel, Noah, Abraham, Isaac, Jacob, and Moses are familiar names most of us may recognize. Yet, some may not recognize Enoch, but God knew him. Enoch became the father of Methuselah at the age of 65. After the birth of his son, Enoch walked with God for 300 years according to Genesis 5:22. Although he had other children, Enoch did not stray from walking with God. God was so pleased with Enoch that He allowed him to bypass physical death. Genesis 5:24 says, "Enoch walked with God; and then he was no more, because God took him away."

Nothing is impossible for God. When His people have faith in Him, they can accomplish mighty things. Under the leadership of Moses, the Israelites left Egypt after 430 years in captivity. Exodus 13:18 says, "God led the people around by the desert road toward the Red Sea." Mountains to the left, desert to the right, and Pharaoh pursuing them. Yet Moses was not afraid. He trusted God to provide a way of escape for his people. God did. By faith, the Israelites passed through the Red Sea on dry ground.

Although the Israelites escaped battle with the Egyptians, there were still more enemies to defeat. When attacked by the Amalekites, Moses stood on a hill with the staff of God in his hands. Exodus 17:11 says, "As long as Moses held up his hands, the Israelites were winning, but whenever he lowered his hands, the Amalekites were winning." Moses realized that victory comes from God. By faith, Aaron and Hur held Moses' hands up until Joshua defeated the Amalekites.

After Moses' death, God chose Joshua to lead the Israelites into the Promised Land. Joshua 6:2 says, "The LORD said to Joshua, 'See, I have delivered Jericho into your hands, along with its king and its fighting men.'" Joshua obeyed God's instructions for the defeat of Jericho. By faith, the walls of Jericho fell.

Five Amorite kings joined forces against Israel. Joshua 10:8 says, "The LORD said to Joshua, Do not be afraid of them; I have given them into your hand. Not one of them will be able to withstand you." Joshua believed God's promise. By faith, the sun stood still and the moon stopped at Joshua's request until Israel had defeated its enemies.

By faith, people rose from the dead, raised to life again at the request of the prophets, Jesus, or the apostles. Others, like Isaiah and Paul, were tortured and refused to be released because they desired the better resurrection.

Hebrews 11:36-38 says:

*Some faced jeers and flogging, while still others were chained and put in prison. They were stoned; they were sawed in two; they were put to death by the sword. They went about in sheepskins and goatskins, destitute, perse-cuted and mistreated—the world was not worthy of them. They wandered in deserts and mountains, and in caves and holes in the ground. These were all commended for their faith, yet none of them received what had been promised. God had planned something better for us so that only together with us would they be made perfect.*

People of faith desire God's best. They are not afraid to trust Him in difficult circumstances because they know He is faithful and will keep His word.

## 20TH CENTURY PEOPLE OF FAITH

*Elittie Harvey* (1903-1988) believed in teaching her children as well as all the other children she could reach. She and Nathan, her husband of fifty-eight years, were farmers in Bellville, Texas. However, that did not prevent them from stopping their farm chores to attend church midweek prayer service. Every person in the family, age five and older, participated because they had learned the importance of prayer.

On Sunday mornings, the family gathered around the breakfast table for Scripture and prayer before leaving for church. When the children were older, they read their Sunday school lessons and prayed.

Elittie taught Bible study and Sunday school for the youth. She also directed their choir. To model what she taught, she volunteered in the community, distributed food, and fought to build a high school for African-American teens in the area. The school was built in Sealy.

Although Elittie shared much of her life with children, none of them heard her complain. Praise, not problems, poured from her lips. She trusted God and encouraged others to trust Him. Her children, grandchildren, and great-grandchildren are following in her steps. Some are more committed than others, but they all know the Lord.

Elittie's life made a difference. She dedicated her life to serving the Lord she loved. Even now, her great-grandchildren, whom she never met, reap the benefits of the rich prayer life of her children and grandchildren. They, too, have a love for studying God's Word and telling others about Him.

*Audrey Wetherell Johnson* (1907-1984), founder of Bible Study Fellowship (BSF) International, was born into a Christian family. As we all know, godly parents do not always guarantee godly children. A Christian environment only gave Audrey the information she needed to make a decision for Jesus. It did not change the spiritual condition of her soul. Although God protected her from certain paths, it was still her decision to accept Him.

Audrey presumed herself a Christian because she knew what to say, and she said it—never intending to confess the sins that God brought to her mind. Self-deception does not stop God from knowing our hearts or doing what He says He will do in His Word. Audrey could fool herself, but she could not fool God. For a while, her faith in the Bible and in Jesus fell away. She became an agnostic who pitied her family and their beliefs.

Audrey may have forgotten God, but God had not forgotten her. When she called out to Him in desperation, searching for meaning and purpose in her life, she was forced to confront her belief about Jesus not being God's Son. His virgin birth was a stumbling block. There is nothing impossible for God. He gave Audrey the insight and wisdom needed to make a decision for Jesus. And according to her autobiography, *Created for Commitment*, God graciously answered all her other questions as well.

Audrey's commitment to God and her faithfulness to carry out His Word led her to Bible school, and then to the mission field in China. She ministered through the China Inland Mission. All she experienced and learned, prepared her for what she would do later. Unknown to her, God was refining and equipping her to be His faithful servant.

After leaving the mission field, Audrey decided to visit America on the way home. Because of her health, she was forced to extend her stay. Not comfortable with idleness, Audrey accepted invitations to speak. After one engagement, five ladies asked if she would teach them the Bible.

Five—a small number. Five Americans—not representative of those she normally taught. Five American women who had access to Bibles, great Bible teachers, and wonderful para-church organizations, as opposed to those she had instructed in China. As she prayed and sought God's will in making her decision, He brought Zechariah 4:10 to her mind: "Who despises the day of small things?" Therefore, Audrey accepted their invitation to teach them.

Hundreds of thousands have benefitted from Audrey Wetherell Johnson's teachings to those five women. That small beginning laid the foundation for Bible Study Fellowship (BSF), an international lay organization for men and women desiring to study God's Word.

*Zomaya Solomon* is living proof that God's message gives life to those who receive it, even when delivered by unwilling messengers. Zomaya is Assyrian. Although his ancestors heard God's message of repentance from Jonah—God's messenger to the Assyrian capital city of Nineveh—it did not stop them from believing God and repenting. Their repentance opened the door for future Assyrians to come into a relationship with God through the Lord Jesus Christ.

When Zomaya was a child, a British missionary visited his home in Duhuki, a city in Iraq, and asked permission for him to attend the missionary school in Mosul. Even though permission was denied, Zomaya did attend the French missionary school in Hassake when his family moved to Syria two years later. Homesickness replaced the joy of the opportunity to attend school because of a language barrier. But unbeknownst to Zomaya, God was preparing him for future service by giving him the opportunity to learn other languages.

God always prepares His messengers before sending them into service. Zomaya was no exception. It was not until the fall of his first year at the French missionary school in Hassake that he realized his need for a personal Savior. Recalling the experience, he said, "That Sunday afternoon after the service, we went to the headquarters, and there on my knees, I gave my heart to the Lord. In every respect I had, as a child, lived a moral life but was not a born-again person. I knew I had to make a decision for Christ."

Zomaya is a third generation Assyrian Christian. In fact he joyfully says, "Many Assyrians are born again." He willingly shares God's Word with others, both here and in his old country, Iraq. As long as a person is willing to hear God's Word, Dr. Solomon is willing to take the time to preach it. He and his wife, Nancy, helped start the Arlington Bible College and Institute, a four-year degree program, while they were members of Arlington Baptist Church in Baltimore, Maryland.

If Jonah had foreseen the spiritual impact of Assyrian Christians in the world, he may have rejoiced to be selected to deliver God's message of repentance to Nineveh.

**Fred Littauer** (1929—2002), husband of Florence and father of Lauren, Marita, and Fred Jr., did not come into a true relationship with the Lord until after twenty-one years of marriage, but once he made that commitment, no one could stop him from helping others or serving the Lord.

When Fred and Florence came to the Lord in 1965, they immediately opened their home and hearts to others—offering their friends an opportunity to know God. Even though they were not Bible scholars, what they learned, they shared. Together, they worked for the Lord—Florence, with the gift of words, and Fred, with the gift of management and compassion.

Fred's primary role was helping his wife, Florence, accomplish her speaking, writing, and teaching ministry after it blossomed. She needed a manager, and Fred chose to be her manager. His attention to details and ability to organize allowed Florence the freedom to pursue her God-given gifts. Although Fred enjoyed helping Florence, God was paving the way for him to have his own ministry within Florence's ministry.

While sharing with others, God allowed someone to minister to Fred where he uncovered childhood trauma. This opened the door for him to acknowledge his victimization and seek healing from the memories. God answered Fred's prayer and freed his mind from the memories that bind. This freedom helped Fred to investigate the memories, accept his past pain, overcome the guilt associated with abuse, receive healing, and share his journey with others.

Some have a difficult time believing God can forgive the sins they have committed or that have been committed upon them. But what about the victims of sexual abuse? They feel dirty outside as well as inside. Even though they are told that the blood of Christ cleanses them from sin, it is hard for them to accept that they are cleansed outwardly and inwardly. But they are. Like all believers, their bodies as well as their consciences are cleansed. They are made whole so they can know, love, and serve our living God.

Fred accepted his outward and inward cleansing. This was the hope he offered other victims of sexual abuse. Instead of being bound by bitterness and resentment, Fred had peace of mind. He freely shared God's love with all he encountered. He wrote *Freeing Your Mind from Memories that Bind* that sold 100,000 copies its first year. He followed it with *The Promise of Healing* and then *Touched by the Master.*

The radiance Fred had for the Lord was so aglow that strangers would ask, "What's different about you?", or even, "How come you are so happy?" He was a beacon to the flight attendants on American Airlines and was responsible for many finding the Lord in a personal way. Nothing is impossible with God—Fred Littauer was a living example of that statement.

African-Americans and whites attended St. George's Methodist Episcopal Church in Philadelphia in 1786, worshiping together freely. Then one day the white members decided that blacks should sit in the balcony. To make things worse, instead of communicating their decision ahead of time, white members tapped their African-American brethren on the shoulders during opening prayers and demanded that they move to the balcony immediately.

**Richard Allen** (1760-1831), an ex-slave and member of St. George's, had a passion for the Methodist Church. His zeal had led to other blacks joining the congregation. **Absalom Jones** (1746-1818)was an Episcopalian. Both were hurt and angered by the treatment they received. They, along with the other African-American members, walked out. But eventually these two godly men joined forces, and the African Methodist Episcopal (AME) Church was born.

History is full of those who have not hesitated to live their lives wholeheartedly for Christ in whatever role He placed them—mothers, educators, preachers, and businessmen. Ordinary people choosing to serve the God who loved, called, and saved them.

Who can deny the faithfulness of Mahalia Jackson, Jenetta East Howard, Susanna Wesley, Marian Anderson, James Montgomery Boice, J. Vernon McGee, Ray Stedman, Francis Schaeffer, A. W. Tozer, Corrie Ten Boom, Payne Stewart, Phillis Wheatley, Thomas Dorsey, Sojourner Truth, R. G. LeTourneau, George Washington Carver, Eric Liddell, Reggie White, Martin Luther, George Whitefield, John Wesley, Dwight Moody, James Weldon Johnson, Harriet Tubman, Peter and Catherine Marshall, Clarence Simmons, Jr., Henrietta Mears, Martin Luther King, Oswald Chambers, Amy Carmichael, Charles Finney, Fanny Crosby, C. S. Lewis, Elma Lee Haynes, Jim Elliot, Andrew Murray, or David Livingstone?

God still calls those who have a heart to hear Him. Do not fail to hear His call.

---

After accepting Jesus Christ as our Savior and Lord, we become vessels of honor, sanctified and useful to the Master. There is no need to compare ourselves with others or seek to be like them, because we are valuable to God just as we are. As long as we submit to Him and are obedient to His Word, He can use us to bring about His will on earth.

Having a relationship with God gives us purpose in life. Our desire is no longer to please ourselves, but rather our desire is now to please God. Regardless of the type of vessels we are—clay, wooden, silver, or golden—we can make a difference in the world.

Are you ready to become God's vessel of honor? Call on Jesus for salvation. Persevere in studying to know His Word. Submit to Him in the circumstances He allows in your life. Surrender completely to His will.

Choose to serve God and others.

# ENDNOTES

## Chapter 1: Identifying God's Vessels

1. W. E. Vine, Merrill F. Unger, and William White, Jr., *Vine's Complete Expository Dictionary of Old and New Testament Words*, (Nashville, TN: Thomas Nelson, 1985), p. 545.

2. *New Illustrated Webster's Dictionary of the English Language Deluxe Edition*, (New York: Pamco Publishing, 1992) p. 853.

3. Ibid, p. 1038.

## Chapter 2: Clay Vessels: Hard to Distinguish from the World

1. W. E. Vine, *Vine's Complete Expository Dictionary of Old and New Testament Words*, p. 545.

## Chapter 3: Don't Give Up!

1. *New Illustrated Webster's Dictionary of the English Language Deluxe Edition*, p.1110.

2. W. E. Vine, *Vine's Complete Expository Dictionary of Old and New Testament Words*, p. 311.

## Chapter 4: Wooden Vessels: Overcoming Others With Scripture

1. Ibid, p. 552.

2. Merrill F. Unger, *Unger's Bible Dictionary*, (Chicago: Moody Press) p. 831.

3. *New Illustrated Webster's Dictionary of the English Language Deluxe Edition*, p.541.

## Chapter 5: Problems: Who Needs Them?

1. Ibid, p. 960.

2. J. I. Packer, *Knowing God*, (Downers Grove, IL: InterVarsity Press, 1993), p. 37.

3. Ibid, p. 37.

4. *New Illustrated Webster's Dictionary of the English Language Deluxe Edition*, p. 173.

5. W. E. Vine, p. 97.

## Chapter 7: Surrendering to God

1. *New Illustrated Webster's Dictionary of the English Language Deluxe Edition,*
   p. 971.
2. W. E. Vine, p. 382.
3. Ibid, p. 382.
4. Ibid, p. 222.

## Chapter 9: They Chose to Serve

1. Vina Harvey Coleman, in discussion with the author, November, 2004.
2. A. Wetherell Johnson, *Created for Commitment,* (Wheaton, IL: Tyndale
   House, 1982).
3. Zomaya Solomon, in discussion with the author, March, 2002.
4. Florence Littauer, in discussion with the author, October, 2004.
5. Rev. Richard Allen, www.members.aol.com/klove01/richalln.htm, August
   19, 2004.
6. Absalom Jones, www.satucket.com/lectionary/Absalom_Jones.htm, August,
   17, 2004.

# *Becoming God's Vessel of Honor*
## Order Form

**Postal orders:**   PO Box 334
Columbia, MD 21045

**E-mail orders:** www.lessieharvey.com

**Please send *Becoming God's Vessel of Honor* to:**

Name: _____

Address: _____

City: _____   State: _____

Zip: _____   Telephone: (_____) _____

Autographed Copy — Yes    Name_____
(Please Print)

**Book Price: $14.99**

**Shipping:**   $3.00 for the first book and $1.00 for each additional book to
cover shipping and handling within US, Canada, and Mexico.
International orders add $6.00 for the first book and $2.00 for
each additional book.

### Or order from:
### ACW Press
### 1200 HWY 231 South #273
### Ozark, AL 36360

### (800) 931-BOOK

or contact your local bookstore